<u>What readers are saying ab</u>

"Finding a good resource on making
to multi-unit management just got a lot easier wiui Cinistop..
book 'The Leader of Managers'. This is a resource that would help any person
moving into multi-unit management understand the vast differences they will
encounter as the take on the challenge of overseeing a number of different
restaurants and begin to experience off-site management. The Leader of
Managers is written by someone who knows both the academic and the "real
world" of restaurant operations and is a welcome addition to a restaurant
company's development program."

Dennis Lombardi, Executive Vice President, Foodservice Strategies,
wdpartners.com

"…an insightful look at the role of the multi-unit manager ... This book is long
overdue and gives all organizations (even small start-ups) an opportunity to
see the progression that can be made from a single unit manager to being the
"leader of managers". The book is set up in a clear, understandable way and
can help new managers, new multi-unit managers, as well as CEOs,
franchisees, and franchisors as the concepts apply to all roles in a business.
The best thing about the book is the application for any type of business, not
just restaurants, but retail and any service as well. This book will be required
reading for all of my classes, as well as any organization that I consult with.
Well done Dr. Muller, well done!"

Robin B. DiPietro, Ph.D. Assoc. Professor & Director, The International
Institute of Foodservice Research and Education, University of South Carolina

"Chris Muller demonstrates yet again that he both understands the
Management and Leadership responsibilities of Multi-Unit Managers and can
act as a translator of academic theory into action. He encourages people to
embrace these ideas and inspires them to become truly world class operators."

Lee Sheldon, Learning & Development Director, SSP Group, UK

"I just finished reading da book!! Enjoyed it very much. Going to have all my
VP's read it beginning Monday"

Ralph W. McCracken, President & COO, Dick's Last Resort

The Leader
of
Managers

Leading in a Multi-Unit, Multi-Site and Multi-Brand World

Christopher Muller, Ph.D.
With Michael Muller

An invitation to readers:
We look forward to your comments, observations and stories about
being a *Leader of Managers*,
or if you are interested in a presentation or seminar,
please send a message to our website:
www.LeaderofManagers.com

Soft Cover
ISBN 978-1-300-85926-0

Hard Cover
ISBN 978-3-300-85750-1

DEDICATION

After all these years of talking to them about it, I must of course dedicate this book to my family—my loving wife Melinda, and my three adult children Lizzi, Michael and Mackenzie—who are always supportive, even if they don't always know exactly which of my latest eccentricities they are supporting.

Christopher Muller
Boston, Massachusetts, USA

CONTENTS

Figures

INTRODUCTION

For more than a quarter of a century I have been fortunate enough to study leaders and managers in the multi-unit restaurant industry. I have listened to and shared ideas with company executives and independent franchisees from dozens of the world's top companies.

In 1992 I helped plan the strategic training program for the growth of Asian management and franchisee development with what was then PepsiCo Restaurants International, what is now YUM! Brands. From 2001 to 2002 I served on a small team of industry experts working with then CEO John Dasburg to re-brand Burger King in anticipation of it being sold by Diageo. I have also spoken to leadership teams from industry leader McDonald's. I have instructed and coached newly appointed restaurant general managers, as well as senior leadership, in the Darden Corporation.

I have also learned from and instructed the managers and senior operations teams of several leading international companies, such as the U.K.'s multi-brand operator Mitchells and Butlers, the innovators at Wagamama, Russia's leading multi-concept operator Rosinter, and the global travel food experts of SSP. I have spent decades conducting seminars for and participating in conferences with dynamic leaders from dynamic companies hailing from such countries as Germany, Sweden, Mexico, Costa Rica, South Korea, and Singapore.

That is to say, I have spent the greater part of my adult life crossing time zones, gathering information from individuals and company leaders in the multi-unit world. During this time many things have changed, not just in the industry but also in society and the economy generally. This is true in nearly every corner of the world.

However, one idea, which is for me a principle, has continued to be relevant: that just as anyone can become a competent manager, also anyone can be a leader; that in today's marketplace, which is dominated by multi-unit, multi-site and multi-concept organizations, we must find, keep, and develop individuals who are at once great managers *and* great leaders.

It is my goal that this book will introduce *you*, the interested reader, to the breadth of challenges, possibilities, opportunities and risks involved in managing multi-unit enterprises. Multi-unit managers are still the same professional knowledge workers who

DEFINING MULTI-UNIT ROLES

The **multi-unit organization** (often called a "chain") is any enterprise or organization that has three or more strategic operating units controlled by a single corporate or headquarters management staff.

The **unit manager** (also called a "general manager" in the U.S.) has responsibility for the daily operation of a single independent business entity, such as one restaurant.

The **super-operator** is directly responsible for the daily operation of more than one business unit which he or she then tightly controls as if those combined units were a single operating entity.

The **multi-unit manager** (sometimes called a "district" or "area" manager) is any individual with direct responsibility for three or more strategic operating units within an enterprise or organization.

The *leader of managers* is not only responsible for independent business unit operations but also for developing the people who manage those units— hence the role is leading and managing other managers.

Peter Drucker referred to in 1954 as the "managers of managers." But the market has changed in the past sixty years, and these positions have evolved with it. Based on my experience I believe that we should now develop multi-unit managers into "*leaders of managers*" and that business owners and company executives should insist that their multi-unit managers learn about and adopt this sophisticated role.

This book is organized into four parts. **Part One** is a broad discussion of the multi-unit **Market** in general, including a brief history of the growth of the multi-unit economy; **Part Two** tackles the multi-unit leader as an **Individual**; **Part Three** covers in greater detail the basic **Organization** of the multi-unit enterprise, and **Part Four,** as an **Application,** is a look into points of intersection between the individual and the organization. This application is meant to illustrate the transition necessary to move from being simply a manager to being a great manager who is also a great leader.

Part One will be most relevant to the reader who takes an interest in a "macro" view of historical and organizational trends. It begins with a look at why the multi-unit, or "chain," organization has been such a powerful force in the modern post-war economy, and concludes with a look at some models of multi-unit competition.

For the reader looking to become, or to aid someone else in becoming, a multi-unit leader, **Part Two** will be of immediate benefit. In this section we explore the idea that the multi-unit manager must be transformed from being a player into a coach, from an actor to a director, or a solo performer into a conductor. I use two complementary but differently researched business models here, the **5 Phases of Leader of Managers Development** and the **Eight Key Success Areas for Multi-Unit Managers**, to illustrate the concepts presented. Then I suggest that there needs to be a real balance struck between management and leadership roles.

If you are, say, a company executive, and you are expecting to lead your team's implementation of its strategic growth plan, you may want to go directly to **Part Three**. In this section I argue that the perspective of leaders in smaller companies differs from that of leaders in multi-unit companies on five key points—Size, Branding, Culture, Power, and Lifecycle. This is also where we look at the "Black Hole" of the Lifecycle, which is worth noting especially by leaders at young companies that are just beginning a stage of rapid growth.

The concluding section, **Part Four**, is a discussion of the importance of how we conceive of management and leadership, in which I argue that we shouldn't consider them to be opposed, or even as two points on some meter of progress. Rather, we ought to recognize that, as our organizations develop, we will, all of us as members of a team, play both roles—manager and leader (and, if we're going to be honest, probably also administrator). Sometimes we are made to play all of our roles simultaneously, at which times we can determine which is to be emphasized only when a challenge or situation presents itself.

It perhaps ought to be noted that in this book I have primarily used restaurants as my examples of real-world multi-unit businesses. I've done this not only because much of my practical experience has been in restaurants and with restaurateurs, but also because multi-unit restaurant companies make up the largest segment of the retail industry in the United States, and they continue to grow as a proportion of all retail organizations. In 2013 they will account for well over 50% of the estimated $650 billion the U.S. foodservice industry will capture.

This sustained growth, both proportional and absolute, and the organizational complexity this growth entails, create an enormous opportunity for well-trained and qualified multi-unit restaurant managers. Franchising continues to be the fastest and surest form of restaurant ownership in the global market, and all companies that sell or lease franchises need multi-unit managers if they intend to grow.

Still, if you are reading this from a perspective outside the restaurant industry, keep an open mind. It should become apparent as you read that all the principles and applications I have used are readily transferrable to other retail business types. I believe everything in this book applies equally well to multi-unit businesses in other segments of the market, such as convenience stores, drug stores, banks, jewelry stores, book stores, equipment rental stores, hotels and specialty retail clothing stores.

Multi-unit enterprise takes many forms. A certain business may be family owned, passed down through two generations, and yet have several units across several counties that serve diverse demographics. A multi-unit company may be publicly traded or privately owned, a franchisor or franchisee; it may operate under management contract, or it may be organized as a partnership. All that these organizations have in common is their complex structure, and the fact that they measure success differently than single-unit organizations do.

Ask yourself this—which of these should your company prioritize in its plans for growth: creating strong market demand, increasing organization size and complexity, broadening distribution channels, enhancing consumer brand awareness, or financing and taking on risk? Though distinct from one another in theory, they are too closely related in practice to distinguish between them. It is the role of the *leader of managers* to gain competence in each of these key areas, in order that he or she can synthesize their competing metrics and thereby help your enterprise grow most effectively.

All retail businesses face the same basic questions when they look to expand from their single-unit.

In this book, I will offer answers to these questions, all while recognizing that the beginning and the end of planning multi-unit growth can often seem to be the very same place.

ACKNOWLEDGMENTS

I need to thank many people for their support and assistance in my multi-decade long work to write this book. Management writers often suggest that we all benefit from having a mentor early in our careers. I have been blessed to have many, certainly more than my share. In no particular order, for each has been important in their own way, let me single out the late "Dutch" Venuti, Tony Hughes, Robert Chase, Avner Arbel, Vance Christian, Stephen Mutkoski, Gretel Weiss, Herwig Niggemann, Doug Doran, and Robin DiPietro. I am grateful to you all for the patient lessons you have given to me.

Some of these mentors have also been my co-conspirators in getting this book to completion but to their names I would like to add Joe Hayes, Ron Shaich, Lee Sheldon, Dennis Lombardi, Andreas Karlsson, Douglas Reeves, David Bosshart, and Terry Varner.

I want to add a special acknowledgement to thank my two "editors"—Michael during the months of writing and Melinda for the sprint to the finish line.

Part One
THE MARKET

1

The "Chaining" of the Marketplace

Four Ages of Segment Evolution
1940-2013

Often referred to as the post-war period, the second half of the 20th century has been an age characterized by increased rates of human migration, by greater integration and liberalization, by a rapidly spreading interdependent, global economic system, and by the much discussed but still under appreciated advancements achieved in industrial and information technologies. Since 1945 we have witnessed a near complete global economic transformation, especially in the retail and service industries. The end of the Cold War and the consequent disintegration of the

Eastern Bloc only reinvigorated the liberalizing process, and the eastern and southern hemispheres have, for some years now, in fits and starts, been participating in the West's modern economy. We hardly need to remind the reader of the growth of Asian and South American economies in the past twenty years.

Over the course of this comprehensive economic overhaul, which began with the end of World War II, the restaurant industry in the United States also changed dramatically. In 1945 the industry was still dominated by locally owned and locally operated single-units, which were typically regulated by a simple ledger in the back room tracking paid and unpaid tabs. The "business of restaurants" has been taking shape, evolving, for more than half a century. Today, in 2013, the restaurant industry is driven by larger corporate entities that employ advanced marketing and organizational techniques in pursuit of a maximized market share.

> The "business of restaurants" has been taking shape, evolving, for more than half a century.

But though these corporations may be responsible principally to shareholders, nevertheless, at the end of the day, they are still more *directly* responsible to their local units. Each of these units serves a community with particular geographical and demographical characteristics, and each of which demands careful, specialized attention in addition to the normalized and standardized guidance handed down from the corporate offices.

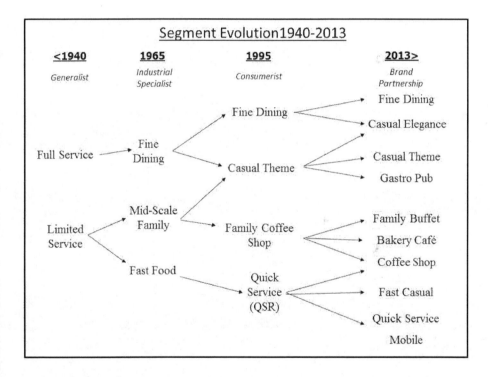

Figure 1

The global restaurant industry is still coming of age. As it matures at different times around the world, cycles in historical restaurant development should naturally repeat as they follow the development of overall worldwide consumer markets, even if those cycles are shortened by the rapidity of knowledge sharing in a digital age.

A new generation of restaurant leadership is developing entire strategies for growth based solely on an interpretation of this new reality. They recognize that in this environment, in order to form successful relationships with loyal customers, they need to focus greater attention on crafting strong brand identities that are flexible and dynamic enough to translate into the idioms of diverse settings. It is in this environment that the role of the *leader of managers* has come to the fore, to the point that we could now argue it is indispensable for the success of a multi-unit enterprise.

I have classified the years between 1940 and 2013 in terms of the dominant figures of the period in the retail industry, particularly the restaurant business (see **Figure 1** above). The first set of these, which designates the more than twenty years between 1940 and 1965, I call the age of the **Generalist.** The second includes the years from 1965 to 1995; I call it the age of the **Industrial Specialist.** The third, the age of the **Consumerist,** is ours, or, at least it has been. I will conclude by arguing that, in

2013, we are entering a fourth age, one which incorporates elements of the preceding ages in interesting and unexpected ways. This is the age of the **Brand Partnership,** and it is in the context of this age that we recognize the real importance of the *leader of managers.*

1940-1965

The Age of the *Generalist*

The end of World War II was not only the dawn of the atomic age; it also marked the beginning of a new commercial age.

Even though by the 1960s many banks and industrial empires had already tested the waters of globalism, nevertheless, in the years between 1940 and 1965, the retail industry remained relatively stable. Retail trade in this period was still considered a form of income substitution, and the market continued to be crowded by single-units, owned and operated locally by independent shopkeepers and small businesses. In this time of great uncertainty about the fate of the world, retail stayed local.

This is no less true for the restaurant industry. Between 1940 and 1965, the U.S. restaurant market was dominated by independent, full-service, family-owned single-units. These restaurants strove to serve "all things to all people," understanding their customers as having broad but uncomplicated needs.

During this period, full-service restaurants often claimed to serve "Continental" menus that offered dozens of items, at least one of which was sure to attract any standard customer. In this sense they were not unlike the more modest but ubiquitous diners that characterize this age in the popular imagination, which employed a system known today as "customized short-order" cooking. This system allowed them to maintain volume and accelerate turn-around while not having to sacrifice breadth of choice.

The nature of these units, and of the market in which they competed, engendered in their owners and operators no great impulse to expand. Likewise, there was very little reason to standardize a unit's system, as no one was likely to replicate the structure of a particular restaurant or retail enterprise in another location. Whatever system was in place was practiced out of habit or superstition, and inertia for the most part kept business stable. As the owner of such a business, you banked on your strategic market position (often meaning a corner location) and did little to test the waters of the open market. There was limited belief that restaurants could reach "scale" and reap the benefits of modern production systems.

I call this period the age of the **Generalist** because it was a time when the market favored restaurants offering comprehensive menus, restaurants that strove to serve some abstract, universal customer whose needs were familiar but wide-ranging. This period also saw the rise of large department stores, of the A&P and other regional food supermarkets, and the continued, though declining, relevance of soda fountain pharmacies and general store lunch counters.

There were, of course, exceptions to the general trend. Fine dining still catered to the tastes of an elite niche, and top chefs in this period continued to combine and test old recipes to discover new ones. More portentous an aberration, however, was Howard Johnson's, which had been founded in the 1920s and which by 1960 had become the world's largest food service company. It was joined in these years by Bob's Big Boy, Friendly's, and Denny's, which were also standardized adaptations of the independent diner model.

It is true that by 1965 these and a few other companies had already taken the first steps on the path to a mature multi-unit structure, but, in terms of total market acceptance, they were far less significant than the multitude of "mom and pop," chef/patron, locally owned and operated restaurants that characterize the period.

Needless to say, in this environment there was, as yet, little demand for the skills of a *leader of managers*. But it is also true that a new form of restaurant organization was on the horizon.

1965-1995

The Age of the *Industrial Specialist*

As we know, the U.S. economy grew rapidly after the end of the Second World War. Great consumer faith at this time was placed in the principles of "American Management" and in the belief that all market activities could and should be industrialized. This meant a belief that hitherto pre-industrial segments of the economy could be made more efficient by the application of empirically sound scientific principles. Solution-driven industrial managers led the application of these principles in highly specialized fields. This was the age of Levittown home construction, General Mills consumer product manufacturing, Madison Avenue advertising and Coca Cola distribution.

The retail industry and the restaurant business in particular caught up to this shifting reality sometime in the late 1950s. By 1965 we see emerge the characteristics of a distinct period, the age of the **Industrial/Specialist**. The worst-kept secret at this time was getting out: all a restaurant company had to do to get its feet on the ground was take a single center-of-the-plate menu item—a hamburger, fried chicken, pizza, ice cream, donuts, fish, roast beef—apply to its production a few industrial techniques and an efficient management system, and then appeal to a "mass market" via television by promising convenience at the lowest price.

In a Darwinian frenzy, new concepts came, set the market on fire, and then quickly shrank or consolidated. In order to compete during this period, a restaurant had to increase capacity in order to meet rapidly growing demand (scale), which consequently lowered operating costs (marginal cost efficiencies), which created even greater profits (increasing marginal revenues) and still broader market demand (scope). It was the perfect industrial circle.

Franchising, which had been used effectively by General Motors to distribute automobiles, became the new "it" ownership model. This was the golden age of "Fast Food," a period during which the industry was dominated by the coupling of a production mentality with a "have it (y)our way" appeal. Concepts that could be systemized were at a premium, as they allowed for a rapid increase in the distribution of brand-name units, and could use "other people's money" to finance this growth.

This is the period when the role of the multi-unit manager as "super-operator" became of great importance (see Chapter 2), especially in the restaurant industry. Specialists in franchise development were in high demand, as they were trained to maintain and enforce standard operating systems. For the individual franchisee, compliance with centralized policies and procedures was the only way to stay a part of an increasingly profitable system. The most successful franchisor organizations were only interested in creating standardized offerings so the mass-market consumer would be satisfied no matter where their purchase was made within the system. The idea wasn't to acquire personnel who could manage other managers, let alone *lead* other managers, as it was to limit variation from an acceptable norm.

1995-present

The Age of the *Consumerist*

The Baby Boomer generation took control of the American economy during the 1980s. Driven by the emerging economic relevance of the Me Generation mentality, by Yuppies' purchasing power and by the consumer rebirth that was Reagan's "Morning in America," markets matured as consumers became increasingly sophisticated. Consumers were also becoming increasingly diverse. For a time, choice and selection seemed to be more important to the consumer than price. A new demand structure was emerging across all retail segments, a "pluralism of demand." We entered a new age dominated by the **Consumerist**, who could respond and cater to the diverse set of consumers' self-identified wants and needs.

"Mass market" at this time was overtaken by "mass customization," as production efficiencies now aimed at offering a "postponed differentiation" experience. Unanticipated lower production costs from this breakthrough created corresponding lower frontline menu prices. This in turn created greater consumer demand, as the happy customer hungered for more and better experiences, which pushed companies to increase capacity again. This was the age of the shopping mall. Specialty retailing rushed to fill spaces as they opened, implementing segmentation strategies aimed at appealing to finer and finer niches of consumers.

The restaurant industry's participation in this general trend is best represented by the development of the Casual Theme, or "eatertainment," segment. No longer was it enough to take that one menu item, like the hamburger, surround it with an efficient franchise and production system, and market it to an undifferentiated mass. Now companies were designing concepts which were story-driven, or ones that offered eclectic, ethnic cuisine.

In the blink of an eye, a consumer could now order fettuccine in a white wine sauce at an Olive Garden on Monday, a Southwest chili burger at Chili's on Tuesday, a deep-dish Chicago pizza at Pizzeria Uno on Wednesday, an authentic "Aussie" steak at Outback on Thursday, a Fisherman's Platter of fried fish at Red Lobster on Friday, a rack of Riblets at Applebee's with the kids on Saturday, and then a rotisserie chicken and warm sides from Boston Market at her kitchen table, brought home for Sunday family dinner. If he were feeling more adventurous, of course, he could swing by Hard Rock Café, or Planet Hollywood, or the more than a dozen imitations of the two, which promised real fictionalized experiences of everything from Motown to magic.

Before Olive Garden, Italian food was considered the domain of the "mom & pop." But by 1992 there were over 60 chains competing in this market segment. One of the reasons Olive Garden was able not only to survive, but in fact to expand, during this period, despite this explosion of competition, was that they relieved stress on their management team by hiring five managers per unit rather than the traditional three. Outback Steakhouse led the industry in outreach to its managing team by offering each general manager the opportunity to be part owner of his or her unit.

A new focus on unit management was required to succeed in this new environment, as these chains expanded from fifty to 100 to 500 units in this short time period. These individual units were now multi-million dollar operations, and they required a more sophisticated management system. The need for a correspondingly more sophisticated *multi-unit* management team became apparent, as there was suddenly dozens of area or district managers in every restaurant organization. To be successful, these multi-unit managers needed to know more than just operations; they needed to understand complex financial, marketing and human resource systems, even if no one was there to teach them these principles.

This segmentation strategy is for the most part the current model for restaurant development in the U.S. However, after the recent extended economic recession, Casual Theme operations are no longer strictly playing the role of specialists, but are in fact now acting more like generalists. We are now looking at the return of the "one size fits all" model. Red Lobster has featured chicken and steak on its menu for years now; Outback offers fish and pasta; Chili's serves not only pizza and pasta, but also tacos and fish; and Pizzeria Uno is now UNO Chicago Grill, with a menu stocked full of steak, pasta and, yes, a few pizzas. After twenty years of success, the Casual Theme segment has matured, and is near the end of its dominance.

Today

The Age of the *Brand Partnership*

The contemporary consumer doesn't make choices based merely on the *product;* she also considers how her choices correspond with her self-fashioned lifestyle. Conspicuous consumers have always wanted their peers to know where they are spending their money, but today they share their choices instantly on a digital chalkboard with a vast, national and international network. Strong brands deliver on the trust their customers put in them. A strong brand can contribute to a consumer's self-actualization, to his level of sophistication, and to his sense that he identifies with an "in-group."

Restaurant prototypes today are blending traditional market segments, creating concepts that are hybrids of fast, casual theme, and elegant, guided by a sense of the importance of consumer-enterprise partnering. We have entered the age of the personal market, of the **Brand Partnership**, and it is characterized by greater specialization coupled with effective customization.

Industry leaders such as Starbucks, Seasons 52, Hillstone, Chipotle, and Panera Bread, all of which blur traditional segment distinctions, are both the product and the agents of this dynamic age.

But even brands such as McDonald's, which has in the last decade introduced and expanded its successful *McCafe* sub-brand (which grew up using older business models) have taken action to adapt to the new environment. While there is certainly significant instability in the economy at large, there is also a feeling of true optimism among some companies, especially among those chains that have been able to take advantage of niche strategies, to build partnerships with their customer base, and to rely on the strength of their brands.

> **It is in this context of complex brand building that a new generation of multi-unit managers is being selected and developed. These *"leaders of managers"* are expected to create high value-added contributions...**

It is in the context of this complex brand building that a new generation of multi-unit managers is being selected and developed. These **leaders of managers** are expected to create high value-added contributions using an entire team of employees across a portfolio of restaurant units. Multi-unit, multi-site and multi-concept restaurant companies are today being designed from scratch with the intention of cornering and exploiting this market. Acquiring sophisticated leadership is a part of this design.

Acceleration of Global Restaurant Forms

The historical trajectory we have outlined in this section, which began in the U.S. after the end of World War II, is today being repeated in Europe, Asia, and the rest of the world. Just as all of the various market forms—the one favoring the **Generalist**, the **Industrial Specialist**, and the **Consumerist**—coexist in the U.S. today, this is also increasingly the case in expanding markets around the world. Time is being compressed everywhere in the world market, and the generations described above are emerging and passing in greater succession in developing economies. This leads to a shortened life expectancy for each generation, but it also accelerates the rate of new development.

The new market environment offers unparalleled opportunities and an almost intoxicating array of consumer choice, and there is the potential to incur enormous profits, as well as enormous losses. In this environment, generalists will still hold on to their traditional, loyal customers, fast-feeders will continue to allow new customers to enjoy the convenience of location and low price, Casual Theme restaurants will continue appeal to the upwardly mobile, and trendsetters will continue to embrace and tackle the new possibilities of branding in unexpected ways.

But at no time in the years we've been discussing have there been better conditions to take advantage of the efficiencies of multi-unit enterprise, whatever form it may take. This market evolution demands of us that we develop a strong team of qualified individuals to lead the next generation of globally minded managers, the *leaders of managers*.

2

The Chained Market

The Advantage of Multi-Unit Enterprise Today

Independent retail enterprises of all kinds are particularly susceptible to the perils of the market. But for years conventional wisdom has held that a higher percentage of restaurants fail than any other kind of retail business. This myth is built on the belief that restaurants are frail when they receive none of the beneficial protection that come from being a part of a large corporate or franchise system.

In 1994 I published an article with Bob Woods in which we argued that this myth was simply that—a myth. Our research showed that independent restaurants failed no more frequently than any other type of independent retail business, and that, in some cases, restaurants as stand-alone units are positioned even more strongly than other single-unit retailers. H.G. Parsa confirmed our findings in 2006.

But we noted also, and perhaps more importantly, that brand name (i.e., franchised) restaurant companies survive in greater numbers than companies in almost any other segment of the retail industry. It is the particular success of this model that we wish to understand with greater depth.

Consider the Portfolio

A good financial expert will tell you that the safest way to invest is to spread your assets among several companies from several different market segments or industries. That way, if one company (or a whole segment) has a bad quarter, the decline in its stock price may be offset by the worth of your other holdings.

That is to say, rather than allowing you to put "all your eggs in one basket," he will encourage you to add long-term stability to your investment by forming a "portfolio." Having the protection of multiple businesses which may or may not follow one another into good or bad periods keeps your investments relatively insulated from the fluctuations of a temperamental and sometimes incomprehensible market.

This principle applies equally well to retail industries. Maintaining a group of branded units in multiple locations shelters a growing company in the same way that having a diverse stock portfolio protects an investor.

In taking this portfolio-minded approach, multi-unit corporations are able to mitigate the risk inherent in any commercial enterprise. Rather than pinning all of its hopes on a single unit, a company can instead invest in various markets with varying demographics and demand characteristics, thus softening the blow of a downturn in any one local market. For example, say you had a great independent restaurant near a thriving industrial site; your business would certainly suffer and could close if the neighboring plant is shut down. But if you have a second unit in an urban financial district, and another by a university, and two more in a small city fifty miles away, the distress felt by the loss of one restaurant is made more tolerable by the continued success of the other four units.

Restaurants in certain popular tourist regions rely on the summer beach season for the majority of their yearly revenues. Management at these restaurants tends to start a round of layoffs during the fall and winter months. The unemployed consequently cut back on spending in these months, leading to a loss of patronage at other local businesses, and the local economy thus enters a spiral of decline.

Many small, independent businesses are woefully under-funded, and any such downturn or short-term loss of business can lead to their complete collapse. On the other hand, if the same local restaurant is part of a larger portfolio of restaurants, perhaps with one unit in a mountain ski region and another in a downtown year-round market, some of the cash flow from these other units can be shifted and re-directed at corporate headquarters to cover the operating expenses of the unit experiencing a seasonal downturn. The risk the entire system takes on is lessened when more units share the burden.

A Depth of Labor Talent

Smaller restaurant companies, many of which are operated by entrepreneurs as sole proprietors, rely heavily on the management talent of one or two people, for example the owner and a trusted associate. These companies are limited by the number of jobs available in a single restaurant. They might employ one or two skilled cooks, one or two competent bartenders, and possibly an eager assistant manager who is waiting in the wings, ready to take on more responsibilities.

But as a system grows, and as an organization becomes more complex, there is likely to develop in it a pool of talent, made up of many people with expertise in multiple areas. Knowledge is acquired and shared across the system. Cooks can be shifted from one restaurant to another where need is greater, assistant managers can be promoted internally, and corporate managers can be cross-trained to broaden their competencies. Informal and formal mentoring opportunities foster the leadership potential of promising employees, and as mentioned before, operating risk declines.

Ray Kroc, the visionary force behind the success of McDonald's, often spoke of the "genius of the system." He was credited as having said, "none of us is as good as all of us." He meant, of course, that his growing company was at its best when it could rely on the more than 2000 franchise owners throughout the McDonald's franchise network to solve unexpected operational dilemmas, to create fresh menu items to meet the needs of local markets, and to identify new talent that would benefit the system in the long run.

Multi-unit companies are also more likely to employ professional managers, who are able to perform what Marcus Buckingham calls one of the key roles of a successful manager, that is, they can control uncertainty and risk. This ensures greater overall stability, and especially for restaurant companies, increases returns on investment.

Larger Cash Reserves

Cash flow is the lifeblood of any sized business. Though rates of cash flow are not equal to profitability, they are directly related. Peter Drucker has said that "profit is the cost of staying in business." Generating cash reserves is the hallmark of well-managed corporate entities.

But whereas a single restaurant might carry a positive cash balance, a company of ten units has the potential to accumulate an account worth ten times what a single-unit can, just as a company operating in 100 or more locations can maintain even greater reserves of cash. The converse, of course, is also true. While a single restaurant might survive with a slightly negative cash balance, a company with ten or 100 units will go bankrupt quickly when that negative balance is magnified by a factor of ten or 100.

If there is a downturn in its local market, the single restaurant faces its cash crisis alone. But in companies with larger reserves, again, the risk is spread, and support can come for individually struggling units in the form of cash that was accumulated elsewhere. Julius Caesar organized his Roman Legion based on this principle. The emblem of his Legion was a bound sheaf of wheat headed by the now familiar saying, "United We Stand, Divided We Fall."

Better Access to Capital Markets

This steady stream of cash reserves increases the likelihood that a company will have easier access to regional or national capital markets. It is the great irony of small business development that it is in fact easier to borrow money when you don't need it as much. There is truth in the cliché that it is easier to borrow $10,000,000 than $10,000. Small independent restaurants often pay higher rates of interest on smaller loans than large companies do on much more significant debt.

In addition corporate restaurant companies have choices when they look to raise capital. They can approach venture capital firms, form equity partnerships, acquire national lines of credit, or make a public offering for the sale of stock in their company to regional or national markets. Access to capital— whether in the form of equity or debt—may significantly lower operating risk. The expansion of either ownership or indebtedness, with a corresponding inflow of cash, provides the potential for rapid growth using "other people's money" or OPM.

An Ability to React to Market Changes

Business models can be either *open* or *closed.* Open models allow customers and suppliers to come and go freely; they allow useful interaction to occur among a broad array of dynamic employees; and they free information to be passed in two (or more) directions. When businesses are closed, on the other hand, they tend to interact with only a small number of well-known suppliers and customers, and they consequently develop an anemic structure for gathering information.

We would argue that to be successful retail enterprises such as restaurants *must* be open. That is to say, they must allow the market, which shifts and dips in ways an individual enterprise cannot control, to drive their businesses.

Multi-unit operations are, by the very nature of their size, particularly susceptible to a wide range of outside market influences. While it is more difficult to control ideas and regulate practices in open rather than closed systems, open systems tend to grow more dynamically because they incorporate a diversity of ideas. When a multi-unit enterprise is well managed, everyone from senior employees to those whose job it is to interact daily with customers can be open to unexpected opportunities that arise from unexpected sources.

The ability to recognize trends across markets, to listen to a wide cross-selection of customers and suppliers, and to respond to what customers are demanding, are the hallmarks of great companies. The more feedback is in the loop the more likely it is that the business will be able to adapt to changes in the market. We have said that cash is the lifeblood of small businesses; we would add to this the idea that new opportunities are food for the beast. If it fails to successfully identify and exploit spontaneously appearing prospects, a business will starve. Having more units which help in the gathering of more information across wider market segments only produces more and greater opportunities, as well as fosters interesting innovations.

The ability of a large, multi-unit corporation to react to changes in local and national markets comes down to the success multi-unit operators have in implementing three key strategies.

First, the operator must commit to **research and development**. In the restaurant industry, this means a commitment to generating new menu items, taking special care to provide items that are on the cutting-edge and are aimed directly at satisfying changing customer desires. In other retail environments, the R & D department is likewise responsible for keeping abreast of consumers' preferences for color, flavor, size, and use. In pursuing this goal, research teams may make use of a laboratory, such as a test kitchen, or of customer surveys and focus groups.

Second, the operator must establish **strong ties to sources of capital**. Financing growth is an essential part of senior management's role in company building. Developing an experienced team of managers who have built relationships with local and national banks, as well as with other capitalizing institutions, is crucial in achieving successful expansion, and this is more likely to occur in a multi-unit company than in a smaller, stand-alone business.

And third, the operator must engage in a process of **advanced environmental scanning**. In performing this role, we might compare this multi-unit manager to a seasoned weather forecaster. A good forecaster spends his time looking out the window at distant horizons, in order to predict what the skies will bring in the next few hours or days. This is analogous to the activity of the market forecaster, who spends his time evaluating the business environment and scans the horizon for bright spots and storms, in order that he can make plans accordingly.

There are, of course, entrepreneurs and owners of small business who have this skill, often intuitively. But in larger multi-unit companies the cost of this activity can be spread throughout the system, thereby increasing the amount of total information that can be gathered. Not unlike how a network of weather stations can report more accurate information to a single forecaster than he could gather on his own, a network of business units can better inform the operator about the nature of the coming market environment. For many years, the Darden Restaurant Corporation had a full time executive, Roger Thompson, who was described by CEO Joe Lee as, "The guy we pay to look around the corner."

Making Economies of *Scale* and *Scope* Work for You

Large, multi-unit organizations have another advantage, what economists call economies of *scale* and *scope*. *Scale* refers to the benefit of increasing the size of an operation, which lowers production costs. For example, a restaurant with twenty seats cannot purchase food and beverages for resale at discount prices. In fact, this restaurant is likely to have to pay a premium for deliveries. A restaurant with 200 seats, on the other hand, is able to buy in bulk or case lots.

The same principle applies to a company with ten units as compared to 100 or 1000. As small retailers grow, they change from holding local to national accounts. With increasing purchasing power, the cost of goods declines and practices of price discrimination begin to take effect.

In general, the marginal cost of producing one additional item for sale will continue to drop as production capacity increases, until the point is reached when the "law of diminishing returns" applies (technically when marginal costs rise above marginal revenues). Since most restaurant firms, unlike manufacturing firms, are constrained by the size of individual units, reaching this point is not typically a concern. However, in Part 3 we will argue that in the "Black Hole" of the life-cycle model, this principle of diminishing returns does take effect.

When a company begins to penetrate the market in such a way that it achieves a relatively dominant position, it can begin taking advantage of its economic *scope*. We measure the scope of a firm based on its reach into a target market. As a company expands, its brand also gains in recognition, thereby increasing the chance that it will continue to expand and at lower risk to shareholders.

As we saw above, companies with more units also have access to additional capital markets; they can gather more information about their own customers as well as those of their competitors; and they are able to establish and enforce organizational efficiencies that smaller companies simply can't afford.

For example, we know that McDonald's has an enormous competitive advantage over its closest competitor Burger King in terms of the amount of resources it is able to spend on advertising. McDonald's has gross revenues that are nearly three times more than Burger King's simply because it operates more units (scope). McDonald's is able to spend almost $800 million per year on advertising and marketing, with the intention of driving up customer count. Burger King, which spends $450 million per year on advertising, is of course at a disadvantage; having fewer real dollars to spend, it is nevertheless required to invest a higher percentage of its annual revenue to keep up (scale). Now consider the local hamburger joint trying to horn in on either Burger King or McDonald's market share. Theirs is surely an uphill battle.

3

Becoming Chained

Knowing When to Grow

There are many reasons why the management of a retail business will feel it is time to grow. The aspiring *leader of managers* will observe carefully both the internal and the external forces putting pressure on her company to expand. By learning to recognize them she may be able to manipulate some, though others will always remain outside her control. Still, to help best lead her single or multi-unit enterprise through its expansion process, she must be able to discern between a sustainable and a forced maturation process.

Recognizing Capacity Constraints

Let's imagine a fairly successful quick-service restaurant concept that is given a break by the construction of a large office complex a short drive away. As the lunch business grows, management recognizes that, with the number of service lines staying the same, many potential customers are approaching the unit for service but are balking at what they perceive to be a long wait-time, and are leaving before making a purchase. In order to meet demand, the manager installs a drive-thru window. But her restaurant is a good one, and it is now strategically located, and the lines continue to grow. Her kitchen facilities are outmatched. Her dining room is too small. At this point, she considers building a larger store, or begins looking into opening a second unit.

In this case, growth is the inevitable result of increased consumer demand.

"Use Them or Lose Them"

An organization might also feel pressure to grow from its "internal customers," that is, its managers and staff. Loyal employees of popular businesses will often seek internal promotion with the hope of taking advantage of strong demand and creating value in a new unit. In this case, a company faces a choice between, as we say, using them and losing them. Decisions made in this situation can mean the difference between keeping highly motivated staff members and watching them slip away, lured by the promises of a competitor. This is an especially hard position to be in for the single-unit operator who is still using an income substitution business model.

Facing a Changing Market

Markets change over time; consumers age and seek to purchase items more suited to their new positions in society; products consequently gain and lose places in consumer's lives. This reality is the foundation of the product Lifecycle model; product and market change is inevitable, and retail organizations need to change along with it.

McDonald's, which has been in business for more than 50 years, is the gold standard in this regard. It has ceaselessly reinvented itself and fine-tuned its business model to stay current. When Ray Kroc and his team began, all McDonald's services were conducted at walk-up windows, which were truly "manned" (the staff was entirely male) in small, single-unit brick buildings. The customer could order just five items—a hamburger, a cheeseburger, a Coke, fries, or a thick shake. Today, McDonald's offers over 100 menu items worldwide, including hamburgers on gluten-free buns, fresh salads, cappuccinos, and low-calorie breasts of grilled chicken.

McDonald's has grown by changing from within to match dynamic change in the market.

Responding to Competitive Pressure

The response to pressure from competitors can occur in one of two ways—it can be either *offensive* or *defensive*. When management decides to add new units in a market thought to be under the control of a competitor, this is an *offensive* growth move. On the other hand, when a competitor looks to enter one of management's home territories, and, rather than looking elsewhere, the management team adds additional units in an already safe area in order to reinforce their control of it, this is a *defensive* growth move. Often this occurs ahead of a more deliberate schedule, as the hope is to capture all future market potential. The former is a classic market penetration strategy, going after territory in a rival's zone in a fight to gain market share. But holding onto existing territory by locking up potential sites of expansion is also sound strategy.

Dealing with Excessive Entrepreneurial Zeal

Sometimes the pressure for growth comes from the owner or founder. The urge to grow, sometimes at any cost, can be a part of this figurehead's vision for his or her company. In his or her zeal for creating something of value, for market dominance, or for seeing a name on the outside of a building, the aggressive entrepreneur can sometimes overlook the dynamics of consumer demand. Growth for growth's sake is a terrible strategic plan, most often because it does not take into account market factors outside of the sightlines of a charismatic leader.

Fulfilling Lenders' and Investors' Demands

Finally, pressure to expand a young company often comes from the individuals most concerned with the fiduciary responsibility of the enterprise, that is, the bankers and lenders who are financing the business. If an aggressive investor bankrolls a company—say, a venture capitalist—the pressure to grow is particularly great. Every lender wants to have a sense that he'll be paid back, and most want to receive a large return on their investment. Either implicitly or explicitly, they may put pressure on management to open additional units sooner rather than later. It is not unusual for outside investors to force companies to expand before they have proven themselves in the market.

Some small or mid-sized companies implement growth strategies because they have reached capacity at a single unit; some do so because they have staff members who are looking to advance internally; others are operating under outmoded business plans and need to revitalize their concepts; others still fear competition, or, rather, fear missing an opportunity to outdo their competitors; some are helmed by a boss with an unflagging mission to dominate, details be damned; and some are steered by overly aggressive guardian angels who are looking to maximize returns on their original investment.

Unfortunately, instead of forging a solid foundation for future growth, many enterprises expand for the wrong reasons. They allow the pressures and the constraints to force them into development, rather than stand strong, thereby granting their enterprises the chance to mature organically and sustainably.

4

Linking The Chain

From Conflict to Unification; From Tension to Alignment

In Part I, we have taken a look at "how we got here," so to speak. We began by outlining, in broad strokes, how changes in society have affected the market at the macro-economic level, with the intention of understanding how our "chained" retail economy came to be as it is. In Section 2 we examined the benefits of multi-unit enterprise in today's risky market. Finally, we described some of the internal and external pressures that encourage management teams to expand, whether or not it's the right time to do so.

In this concluding section, we will pick up on an organizational dynamic alluded to in the previous section, a dynamic which is unique to multi-unit enterprises.

Market Tension

We begin with the traditional micro-economic duopoly, two firms—Firm A and Firm B—competing in any given marketplace (see **Figure 2**). The management of Firm A seeks to maximize profit and sees in Firm B the limit to its doing so. The management of Firm A makes decisions based on its assumptions about what tactical and strategic decisions its competitor is making. The management of Firm B does the same. Each looks out the window and across the street, and thinks, "What is he up to? What will she do next?"

Different Metrics – Different Outcomes

The Conflict Model: Traditional Independent Market Tension

Figure 2

Both management teams will no doubt use their own set of metrics to determine their companies' "profit" (*utility*). While one might want high cash flows, the other might be looking for long-term asset appreciation. Or maybe Firm A measures market share in terms of customer count, and Firm B uses top line revenues to measure share. True, it is typical of small-business owners to be particularly concerned about cost containment, but still, each management team must decide what its firm will sacrifice in order to maximize utility, however it's determined.

But when a company, say Firm A, grows to the multi-unit level, that is, when its infrastructure becomes more sophisticated and when new teams of management spring up among its ranks with new roles and new expectations, the structural complexity of its organization inevitably complicates its way of measuring success. In the figure above, the will of Firm A to increase profits and maximize utility is represented as being controlled by a single directing force. This is because, in its competition with Firm B, Firm A measures success in only one way, namely, in relation to Firm B.

As it expands, however, there emerges *within* Firm A four competing stakeholders. We say these stakeholders are competing, or in *conflict,* because they each measure success in a way that is particular to their position within the organization. Firm A is now made up of four discreet agents with four different ways of determining utility (see **Figure 3** below). Sure, at the end of the day these four might all want what's best for the company, and it might be the case that, in person, the men and women who perform these roles get along fine; but, in the natural course of accomplishing tasks distinctive to their individual roles, they inevitably use metrics of success unique to each of them. In so doing, they unwittingly put stress on the system, stress that, we argue, can only be overcome by a successful "brand alignment" driven by—who else?—the *leader of managers.*

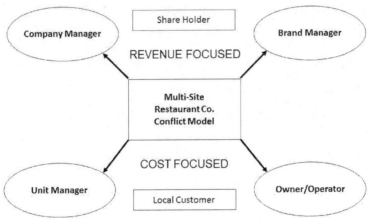

Different Metrics – Different Outcomes

The Conflict Model

Figure 3

Different Metrics – Different Outcomes

While it is the case that the "corporation" is the technical owner of a modern multi-unit enterprise, it's also typically the case that there will be either a franchise agreement between that corporation and a unit owner, or a contractual agreement between it and a corporate unit manager, who may hold an equity stake in his single unit. In the figure above, we mean this individual, the local franchisee, when we refer to the **owner/operator.**

In the multi-unit environment, a **unit manager** and a unit **owner/operator** do not always share a single way of measuring success. Unit managers all over the world determine their success based on how well they have maintained control over the combined cost of goods and labor (what we in the United States call the *prime costs*). A unit manager will most often measure his ability to do so in terms of a percentage, that is, the percentage of gross sales. Any deviation above a standard percentage of prime costs in terms of gross sales and there will be no quarterly bonus.

The owner/operator, on the other hand, is usually more concerned about the need for positive cash flow. She worries about satisfying vendor's invoices, meeting payroll, and covering the rent, and therefore measures her success by counting the dollars she takes to the bank on a given day. She knows that an owner who doesn't pay the bills closes the doors. (It should be noted also that owners will sometimes measure success by assessing the market value of their businesses.).

Obviously, these two perspectives—the unit manager's and the owner/operator's—while both necessary, are not the same. Trying to meet a certain target percentage point may or may not create a positive cash flow, but it will certainly set in motion a series of decisions and plans on the part of the unit manager that will not necessarily consider which way the cash is flowing.

The unit manager and the owner/operator do share a common concern over containing costs. At the end of the day, they both want to ensure that the fewest dollars possible are spent on food and labor. The two operators also both know they need to please their local patrons. A common thought is that 80% of a restaurant's trade comes from within ten minutes travel time, or three miles driving distance. Satisfying this local clientele is the primary motivator of the unit manager as much as it is of the local owner/operator.

What we call the **brand manager** in the figure above is in fact none other than the multi-unit manager. While he is responsible for a multitude of tasks and therefore has many ways of measuring success, the multi-unit manager is most especially held responsible for ensuring the growth in market share of his brand, which he measures in percentages. Likewise, a multi-unit manager might measure the percentage growth in average unit volume (AUV) among her units, or the percentage increase of customer foot-fall, to assess her occupational progress.

The fourth stakeholder, the person in the model we call the **company manager**, is the corporate executive who is focused solely on maximizing shareholder returns. She measures success in terms of company share price by determining after-tax profits per share. She drives dollars to the bottom line. Like the unit owner, the company manager's metric is dollars, not percentages.

Over time, as the marketplace has become dominated by multi-unit restaurant companies, often at the expense of single-unit businesses, the brand and company managers have been responsible for creating a profound change in the industry at large. To meet goals set for them by shareholders who demand increased asset value, sometimes driven by short-term planning in a push for growth these individuals have had to set targets on increasing unit revenues. If revenues rise and marginal costs remain stable, profit as a percentage of total sales will rise dramatically. It is reasonable to suggest that the focus on top-line revenue has come at the expense of the more traditional focus on unit cost containment. This, as we described above, is the more

The Unified Model

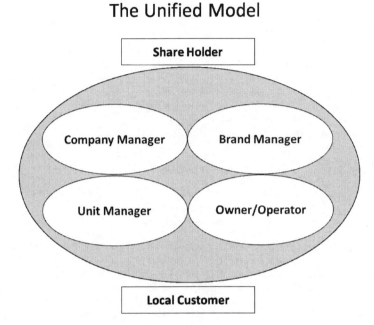

Figure 4

traditional approach to finding profits shared by the unit manager and the owner/operator.

Balanced Perspectives, Balanced Metrics

If local customers are not rewarded for their loyal patronage, profits will not increase and the stock price will not rise either. If owner/operators blindly drive expenses lower, they will eventually see their cash flows dry up. (No guest ever went to a restaurant because it had the lowest food cost in town.) Unit managers cannot lead their staff by simply meeting budgeted labor cost percentages. Brand managers who work solely to expand market awareness and brand identity may wind up managing a stale or diluted brand, and company managers who get all their satisfaction from doling out dividends to shareholders will forget to build something of value, and in the end find that their foundations are not solid and cannot maintain an edge in the market (see **Figure 4** above).

Clearly, unifying these competing stakeholders would be a significant competitive advantage for the well-managed multi-unit company. Because each actor has a unique perspective on success, it can be very difficult for any one of him or her to be expected to step up and to achieve this unification.

It is here that we take a turn and begin describing and defining what makes the role of the *leader of managers* different than other positions in the multi-unit environment. Beginning with a look at this role player as an *individual*, we present the characteristics and tasks that are unique to the *leader of managers*.

Part Two

THE INDIVIDUAL

1

Identifying Leading Individuals

From Player to Coach, Actor to Director, Soloist to Conductor

As individuals in a growing company transform, breaking through the psychological barriers that confine them to a skills and task competency, they will be confronted by the challenge of adopting new behaviors. Just as a great center on a basketball team is not necessarily going to become a great coach, and an Academy Award winning film actor is not guaranteed to become a great director, neither is a "super-operator" always able to free his or her mind from the habits and intuitions of the unit manager and thereby become a *leader of managers*.

Of course there are instances of successful "player/coaches" in professional sports, like the great Bill Russell, and some actors can direct themselves in movies, such as George Clooney and Ben Affleck, still it is rare that someone possesses both sets of abilities and is successful in each realm concurrently. This being the case, I suggest that successful multi-unit managers need to play a role more like that of a coach who draws up the playbook but does not enter the game, or the orchestra conductor who does not sit first chair.

> **"The *leader of managers* engages, encourages and empowers others to play, portray and perform."**

For example, the multi-unit manager ought to be just as competent at completing a monthly staffing schedule as her unit manager. But as the coach/director/conductor she should agree only to *help* with, not *do*, the necessary routine tasks of the unit manager. Rather the *leader of managers* engages, encourages and empowers others to play, portray and perform.

Three Key Leadership Attributes

It ought now to be clear that the skills of a successful unit manager are not identical to those of the successful multi-unit manager, or *leader of managers*. Three attributes—**personal**

motivation, mastery of delegation, and belief in servant leadership—define the difference. Executives should look for indications that these attributes may be present in an individual when identifying people ready to make the leap to the next level. You may ask yourself whether they are present in you, as well.

Personal Motivation

The *leader of managers* understands the difference between motivation by **extrinsic factors** (outside forces) and by **intrinsic factors** (inside forces) [see page 215, **Figure 18**]. The time-sensitive and formalized structure at the unit level often mitigates the kind of procrastination that can paralyze a new multi-unit manager, who must face a highly unstructured and self-scheduled day.

People who thrive in the regular daily cycles of a restaurant will find it hard to figure out what to do when they start their day as a multi-unit manager. Unit managers are surrounded by people seeking their advice and attention; LOMs typically work alone and set their own pace. The *leader of managers* must be a self-starter, willing to work in a nearly unstructured environment, often only responsible for the completion of a personal daily routine. Company leaders need to discover first if this trait is present in an individual before offering a promotion.

Mastery of Delegation

A multi-unit manager must be able to "let go" of tasks, responsibility, and authority. Unit managers might delegate some small stuff, but for the most part they thrive in the role of "boss," making dozens of decisions, large and small, every day. On the other hand, multi-unit managers make suggestions; they succeed by being persuasive, not by giving commands.

The *leader of managers* is able to delegate, to hold others responsible for their decisions, and to give away authority to facilitate smooth operations. Identifying individuals who exhibit comfort in this role will go a long way in accelerating their transition from "super operator" to *leader of managers*.

Belief in Servant Leadership

The third attribute to surface in new multi-unit managers is an attitude of "servant leadership." Whereas top general managers tend to be focused on the staff, they are also driven to succeed on a personal basis, in a way that might be described as "inner directed." Most are highly competitive, not only with themselves but also with other GMs in the system and with other competitive restaurants in their market.

Top multi-unit managers need rather to be "other-directed" and cognizant that their success now depends entirely on the success of the people who they manage. They will naturally begin to exhibit a desire for organizational success, not merely for their own individual achievement. Finding people who exhibit this trait is often not a priority when looking for new multi-unit managers. It ought to be.

2

Developing Leading Individuals

Introducing the "5 Phases"

For more than thirty years, at least since the publication of research conducted by Kimberly & Miles in 1980, there has been agreement at both the academic and practical levels on the usefulness of the "organizational life cycle model." The life cycle model draws a picture of business development as a process akin to the maturation of a biological organism.

The **5 Phases of *Leader of Managers* Development** model, shown below (see **Figure 5**), is an application and adaptation of such an approach. It depicts development as a function of complexity and time. The curved line represents the development of the *leader of managers* (LOM), and on this line we have made marks that designate the achievement of five key competencies—**Operations, Facilities Management, Finance, Marketing,** and

Human Resources. In this section, we will outline the proper progress of a true LOM, and in doing so will come to a better understanding of what distinguishes a *leader of managers* from a typical multi-unit manager, or "super-operator."

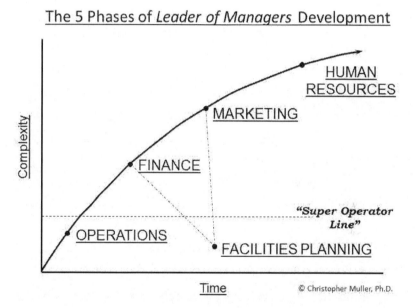

The 5 Phases of *Leader of Managers* Development

Figure 5

Operations

We assume that most, if not all, multi-unit managers have at one time served as single-unit managers. It is often the case that the best and most effective unit manager in a given region will be hired or promoted to the level of multi-unit manager. When he or she moves into this new role at the multi-unit level, this individual is expected to bring along the hard-earned skills and competencies he or she gained while effectively managing a single unit. The transformation of a multi-unit manager into a *leader of managers* can only be accomplished on a foundation of operational competence.

A newly promoted multi-unit manager will often have to work two or three times harder than he did as a unit manager, given that he will continue to perform some of the functions of his old job—concerning himself with questions about staffing, production, and scheduling—while he will now also have to consider the needs of an additional two to four units when making his decisions.

The inevitable increase in stress can stunt the growth of certain individuals. It tends to be the case that in challenging and stressful times we manage to our strengths. We rely on familiar habits. For this reason, it is very natural that many multi-unit managers who are highly competent at the operational level nevertheless get stuck, so to speak, performing the role that we have called the "super-operator."

The "super-operator" is often efficient, but she is not a truly effective multi-unit manager. She is able to control unit food and labor costs, maintain a full staff schedule, drive up customer counts, ensure a safe and well-maintained building, and pass mystery shop inspections. But she is prohibited from further personal development because she can only think tactically. She bases her decisions solely on her own understanding and trust in past successes and projects only into the immediate future.

These decisions, which are often based on intuitions or are a product of habit, may still work for a short-time horizon in a tightly controlled environment. But if the multi-unit manager is to transcend the role of the "Super Operator" he must liberate himself from his preoccupation with daily unit operations and see a bigger picture. He must come to understand that his new job requires a constant and active drive to integrate. He must realize that, as a multi-unit manager, he is responsible for maintaining and then strengthening a cohesive network among his units, of which he is the visionary leader.

Finance

A unit manager will spend her time looking exclusively at unit-level operating income (primarily because her bonus is traditionally based on this line item), and will typically only consider data relevant to a week- or perhaps a month-long planning horizon. The developing LOM must learn to take into account how an investment decision affecting one unit today may have an impact in three or even six months, and how each financial decision rarely affects only one unit but can have an impact on an entire district.

The multi-unit manager must come to see that sound financial management requires more than a concern for the numbers; it also requires carefully allocating scarce resources across an integrated system. She must recognize that profits are not just generated from unit operations, but from wise resource investments in both people and facilities.

It has been said that anyone can cut costs by 10%, but that only a genius can spend money wisely. We would alter this to say, any multi-unit manager can manage costs at the unit level, but only a *leader of managers* can plan for the future of his whole district. By learning to see not only the parts, but also the financial whole, by gaining an awareness of how cash is fluid and flows from an individual restaurant into the district office and then into the corporate headquarters, the multi-unit manager moves that much further along in his transformation into a *leader of managers*.

Marketing

Once she has achieved an understanding of finance, of investment and integration, the multi-unit manager can begin to cultivate a new competency, one which, when mastered, will provide her with a whole new perspective. It is at this point in her development that the aspiring LOM turns her attention from looking inward at the operation to looking outward toward the customer.

Marketing, in all of its components, reaches out to customers where they live and creates in them a desire to become trial users and ultimately committed regular guests. The time spent building a strong operational system will reinforce this desire by providing patrons a reason to return. An LOM is able to recognize and exploit these key points of intersection among operations, finance and guest satisfaction.

At this point in his development, a multi-unit manager must come to internalize the idea that success at the multi-unit level requires a maximization of brand value through marketing and customer retention. Ultimately, his goal must be to gain patrons who identify personally with the brand.

Human Resources

Eventually, after mastering the fundamental competencies of **Operations, Facilities Management, Finance**, and **Marketing**, the aspiring LOM is able to focus on that which is most characteristic of the *leader of managers*—achieving results through the development of other people.

True *leaders of managers* are those individuals who create talented teams, who develop a deep and diverse bench of promotion-ready managers, and who maintain high employee retention rates (and not just low turnover rates) at all levels of employment.

At this point in her journey, which for the best multi-unit managers should take no longer than 24 months, almost all of the work of the LOM is spent investing in the people who truly create customer value—her staff.

The Virtuous Circle

Professional operations lead to solid financial results. Financial strength allows for investment in both facilities and customer outreach through innovative marketing. Targeted marketing builds a strong brand identity that attracts both loyal customers and top performing employees. High achieving team members demand personalized training and development. Completely engaged employees are able to grow to their full potential, and in turn, benefit their professional operations.

When a multi-unit manager is able to balance this delicate and complex ecology, he has become a properly enlightened, effective *leader of managers*.

A Closer Look at the "5 Phases"

Product, Profit, Growth, Retention

So much for the basic overview. On the following page is a complete and fully detailed version of the 5 Phases Model (see **Figure 3**). You will notice the addition of four italicized focal points—*"Product," "Profit," "Growth"* and *"Retention,"*—each of which directly corresponds to the phases outlined above. In addition we have added greater specificity as regards skills competency and concept mastery during each phase.

We offer this more robust portrayal of the 5 Phases model as an action plan. The following discussion is meant to help you or the people you manage fully develop into complete *leaders of managers.*

To help with this concept, this section reveals how each of the transition points must begin with a new perspective on who will do which tasks. These emerging leadership behaviors, as in coaching, are both active and passive activities. Each requires give and take. In this framework the LOM offers and the unit manager accepts shared ownership and responsibility for the outcomes of their collective actions.

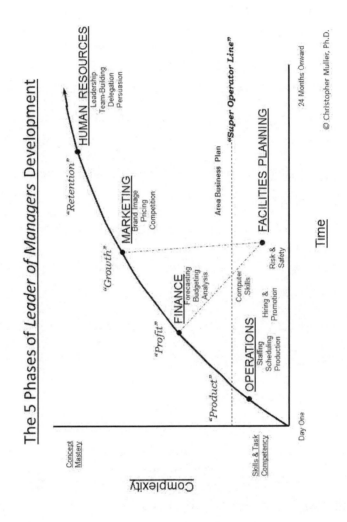

The 5 Phases of *Leader of Managers* Development

HUMAN RESOURCES
Leadership
Team-Building
Delegation
Persuasion

"Retention"

MARKETING
Brand Image
Pricing
Competition

"Growth"

FINANCE
Forecasting
Budgeting
Analysis

"Profit"

FACILITIES PLANNING
Risk &
Safety

Area Business Plan

"Super Operator Line"

Computer
Skills

Hiring &
Promotion

OPERATIONS
Staffing
Scheduling
Production

"Product"

Concept
Mastery

Skills & Task
Competency

Complexity

Day One   24 Months Onward

Time

© Christopher Muller, Ph.D.

Figure 6

As first discussed above and shown here in the model in **Figure 6**, a developmental training program for the newly promoted multi-unit manager should be constructed on the reasonable assumption of personal growth over a period of time. The highlights of this approach include the path from being a "super-operator," or the very accomplished tactical manager, to the more nuanced strategic role of *leader of managers*.

As noted above, when promoted this person exhibited all of the successful traits needed at the unit level by a unit general manager, especially a heavy reliance on the technical operational skills defined by the organization. Now, though, to become successful he or she must learn and exhibit mastery of the more complex management issues of finance, marketing and, ultimately, human resource development.

Phases 1 & 2

Operations and *Facilities Planning*

Many management writers will admonish an advancement-minded managerial candidate to exhibit the skills and competencies of the job they desire. Unfortunately, that is only good up until a point. As the complexity of the new position becomes apparent, typically immediately after being promoted, it is only natural that the new multi-unit manager falls back to exhibiting the attributes and behaviors associated with their previous "comfort zone" of existing skills. These comfort skills include the dimensions of what it takes to be successful in the realm of Restaurant Operations and Facilities Management.

Focusing on the *Product*

In a later section I will detail how the concept of the Restaurant Brand Pyramid requires two foundations—**Quality Products and Services**, and **Flawless Execution**. I call these the "table stakes" which are required for entry into the game, the minimum standards set to be a true competitor in the professional restaurant environment.

The execution of these core Operations activities, summed up in the Ray Kroc mantra—Quality, Service, Consistency and Value (Q, S, C & V)—are all about having the right people in the right positions doing the right things every time a customer is served a meal (see **Figure 7**). Basically, a unit manager's measurement of success might include (but is not limited to) unit-level tasks such as staff and production scheduling, food and labor cost control, daily building maintenance and achieving acceptable customer satisfaction scores.

These are the skills which ensure that unit performance is seen by the customer as the actual *"product"* which is being offered. Indeed, much has been written in the business press about the difference between a manufactured and a service "product" and restaurants are often the leading example of this difference.

I often encourage my international and domestic seminar participants to consider the retail unit on a street corner no differently than they would a consumer product on the shelf in a supermarket aisle.

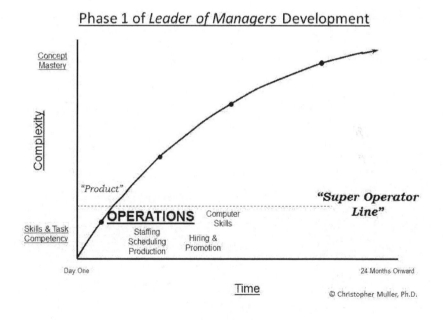

Phase 1 of *Leader of Managers* Development

Figure 7

Consumers ask themselves "what's in the box?" whether the purchase decision is about breakfast cereal or a drive-thru cheeseburger. As long as the product matches the expectations promised by the packaging, the customer is content and management is rewarded.

However, this focus on the restaurant as product tends to emphasis the role of the multi-unit manager as "super-operator." But the mentors of these newly promoted area managers, and the new managers themselves, need to move past this phase as quickly as possible. This requires building on acquired task competencies while knowing that learning new skills and mastering new concepts are required for the LOM to effectively lead other managers.

Granted, the role of the Coach/Director/Conductor includes mastery of specific operations related activities. These tasks are always accomplished by taking action, sometimes physically, such as by visiting units and conducting operational audits, and sometimes more abstractly, such as by analyzing operating results. The coach enforces QSC standards, those measurable outcomes related to product quality, service excellence, and cleanliness. The conductor assures that unit managers and employees understand recipes and production procedures while monitoring the effective use of labor-scheduling techniques.

The director guides unit managers in recognizing and solving operational issues as they supervise the development and implementation of unit operational plans. The coach oversees the gathering of combined operational data for review and analysis.

These roles mean the conductor is expected to lead the unit managers in his or her district towards operational harmony.

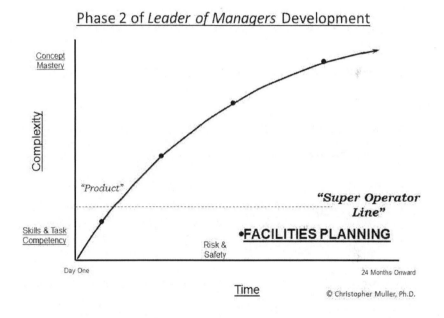

Figure 8

Facilities planning and safety management means focusing on the physical plant (see **Figure 8**). Most managers consider this a necessary but unglamorous activity. As novelist Kurt Vonnegut wrote, "…everybody wants to build, nobody wants to do maintenance."

In reality, mastering the tasks in this area helps to increase competitive value by making company assets worth more through positive consumer brand recognition and customer loyalty. The skillful multi-unit manager, like a defense-minded coach, monitors unit-level security and safety procedures. Multi-unit managers directly supervise preventive maintenance programs and coach unit managers to recognize facilities and safety issues.

While conducting regular performance reviews they approve low-cost immediate repairs to unit facilities and then recommend more costly investment improvements, managing the repair and maintenance budget across all units in the district. Part of this is developing the skills necessary to be able to conduct cost benefit analysis for repair and maintenance proposals from a variety of unit manager demands.

Phase 3

Finance

Even without explicit instruction or specific training, a new multi-unit manager will recognize the importance of focusing on system-wide profits. At this point a personal development program should be reinforced to advance the maturation process, to the benefit of both the multi-unit manager and the company which employs him.

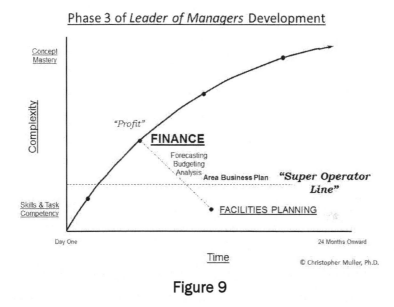

Phase 3 of *Leader of Managers* Development

Figure 9

At this point, the 5 Phases Model becomes more a personal roadmap than a theoretical device (see **Figure 9**). As the new multi-unit manager gains experience and perspective he realizes that the complete financial dimension is more complex than the simple operating P & L statement was at the unit level. To break out of the "super-operator" mindset, a new mastery of the more abstract relationship among profitability, resource investment and guest satisfaction must occur.

Focusing on *Profit*s

In order to drive district-level profits, the multi-unit manager must first understand forecasting, budgeting, and cash flows holistically. This leads to the need for the creation of an **Area**

Business Plan, which synthesizes information gathered from all units into a set of meaningful projections and profitability goals. This plan will take into consideration allocating capital for preventive maintenance, for investment in physical plant and equipment repairs, for marketing expenses, and for the development of a professional team. It demands of the multi-unit manager that he adopt a more expansive decision-making horizon than he would have at the single unit level.

Fundamentally, financial management is about seeing how "the numbers" match the business operation. No company can maintain profitability for long without a reliance on leaders in the field who possess strong analytical, forecasting and budgeting skills. The *leader of managers* must be able to analyze market trends, make exceptions to budgets as circumstance demands, and set investment priorities.

The LOM coaches unit managers to recognize cost variances while she monitors unit level financial performance and also assists unit managers in developing financial and sales forecasts. She guides unit managers in the development of corrective action plans both for staff and operational issues. She oversees compliance with purchasing controls and authorizes expenditures within policy limits.

Phase 4

Marketing

To facilitate district sales growth, a new appreciation for the importance of marketing should be encouraged in the multi-unit manager. Marketing is less skill-based and more conceptual than the previous three phases. Gaining competence at this stage requires an abstract understanding of brand management, of the role of competition in the marketplace, and such issues as pricing, brand strength and the positioning of the district's units (see **Figure 10**).

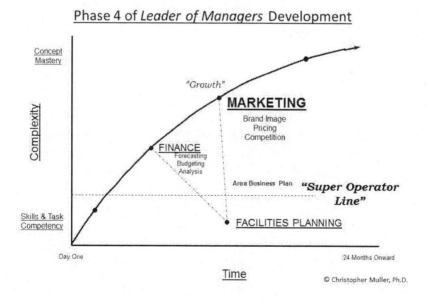

Figure 10

It is reasonable to expect that the experienced multi-unit manager's decision-making horizon has by this time expanded from short-term to mid-term (or, hopefully, longer). It is crucial that this broadened outlook precede a focus on marketing because the implementation of successful brand enhancement campaigns will often require six to nine months of planning and development over multiple sites and neighborhood markets.

Focusing on *Growth*

Marketing is at its core about growing the customer base, both by attracting new trial users and by increasing the frequency of visits and strengthening the loyalty of existing customers. In both cases, the markers of success are different for a multi-unit leader than for a single-unit manager.

Marketing, promotions and brand management are all about finding and keeping the customer. Satisfying the customer, of course, is the first order of business. The practitioner of marketing has at his disposal a number of tools to accomplish this general goal, including setting prices that enhance a positive brand image.

Price management and competitive positioning are crucial, especially in the age of social media. In a service business, very little information about quality is available to the customer until after a purchase is made. However, two things can signal value and positioning to a customer prior to his or her purchase—selling price and location.

The link between marketing and facilities management should, then, be obvious. The planning, site placement and maintenance of the restaurant facility is equivalent to the graphic design and shelf location of consumer goods. Whether on the supermarket shelf or on the street corner, marketing answers the consumer's question, "what's in the box?" which drives the decision to purchase.

It is the growth oriented LOM who supervises new product introductions and develops unit manager's awareness of customer preferences. He monitors in-store advertising programs and promotional plans as he recommends and supervises implementation of local store marketing concepts and programs. As he does this, he helps unit managers develop community relations programs. Ultimately he trains his managers to assess competitor operations, including their pricing tactics and strategies, competitive marketing and advertising campaigns.

Phase 5

Human Resources

Success at the final phase requires addressing the complex conceptual issues of human resources (see **Figure 11**). No *leader of managers* can be fully empowered to control his units

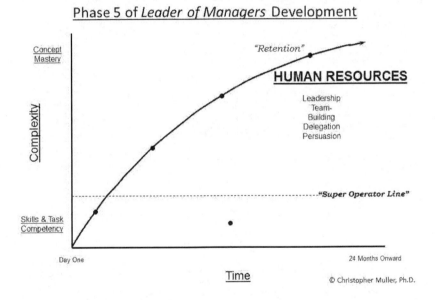

Phase 5 of *Leader of Managers* Development

Figure 11

until he begins to see that his role has evolved from "task master" to "people developer." Companies with multi-unit managers who understand human resources management should expect to see lower unit-level staff turnover rates across their districts, which will directly enhance unit profitability.

Focusing on *Retention*

In addition to longer unit-manager service tenure, companies with development plans for their *leaders of managers* can expect to see higher levels of retention of key employees. Companies learn not to measure the number of marginal people who leave their units, but to focus on keeping and rewarding the good people who stay. The smart leader learns quickly that turnover costs the company money while retention saves money by leveraging a long-term investment in human capital.

The focus for the LOM at this phase is to build deep unit-level bench strength, with high performing teams and collaboration amongst staff both at the unit level and across the district. A good development program would include all the things mentioned above and in addition would inculcate an appreciation for how people learn differently and at different paces, and for how they are differently motivated to succeed.

While the model suggests the path for development could take up to two calendar years, each newly promoted or newly hired *leader of managers* would necessarily proceed at a self-directed pace. An experienced multi-unit manager might hit the ground running and adjust in a month or two while the newly promoted unit-manager might take the full 24 months to fully make the transition. Rarely should this development be allowed to take longer than 24 months.

Ultimately, leadership in business is built on persuasion, not brute force. Leadership is the ability to move people from one place to another, motivating and encouraging them to do things they might not, or cannot, do alone. The mastery of these complex interpersonal skills is the final phase of the *leader of manager's* journey.

The LOM serves as a resource and provides feedback to unit managers. He supervises the execution and implementation of in-unit training and development programs She coaches and motivates both managers and employees and also takes disciplinary action when necessary. He identifies and prepares subordinates, especially emerging assistant unit managers, for future promotion. She supervises and conducts formal management performance evaluations while modeling effective supervisory behavior. He reinforces and rewards the training and development of employees. And, she oversees district-wide analysis of personnel needs and develops staffing plans with individual unit managers.

3

Assessing the Individual

The Eight Key Success Areas

The next model we will use to explicate the complex role of the multi-unit manager is based on research my colleague Robin DiPietro and I conducted in 2005 over the course of a year. Our research at that time indicated to us the existence of eight "areas" that *leaders of managers*, executives, and trainers ought to identify and attend to as they work to move their organizations forward.

We call this model, appropriately, the **Eight Key Success Areas for Multi-Unit Managers**. Whereas the **Conflict Model**, discussed in Part I, was a representation of intra-organizational tension and alignment, and the **5 Phases Model** charted the development of the *leader of managers* as a function of time, this model represents the tension that arises necessarily as the multi-unit manager allocates his limited time and energy. Therefore, this model can be just as useful a guide when setting daily priorities as when determining company-wide benchmarks.

The model is divided into four quadrants that are established along two axes: one we call the **Human Resource Management – Finance** axis, the other, the **Operations – Strategy** axis. Each of the eight areas discussed below has been placed along these axes according to the pull of opposing forces the multi-unit manager experiences as she makes decisions (see **Figure 12**).

The horizontal axis represents the tug-of-war between human resource managers and financial managers as they determine to what extent staffing and training costs can be controlled while maintaining strong customer service. It is often the case that financial managers, in their eagerness to save, view the people in their organization as more dispensable investments than those they have made in facilities, equipment, and materials.

While close attention to a balance sheet is crucial to any profit-making enterprise, never the less "finance" tends to overlook the unintended expenses of high turnover rates and insecurity in the workforce. As morale improves, productivity increases, and competence is rewarded. It is the role of the multi-unit manager to maintain a balance between cost-cutting financial managers and labor-oriented human resource managers.

Similarly, the multi-unit manager faces the opposing forces of Strategy, which takes the long view, and Operations, which concerns itself with today. The agents at either end of either axis may accurately formulate assumptions and may effectively articulate demands, but no one point is complete in itself. Therefore we must get a complete picture of the overall relationship among these four realms. The *leader of managers* knows that Human Resource Management has an impact on strategic decision making, that operational concerns affect financial actions, and so on.

Identifying and assessing individual managers based on how they organize themselves along these two axes offers one the opportunity to see how they set priorities and in particular how they exhibit *balance* in the much more complex working environment of multi-unit management.

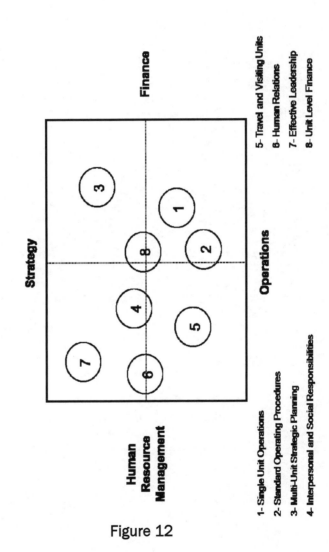

Figure 12

Single Unit Operations

We may start with a straightforward, observable philosophy—you can't hate waiters and cooks and be an effective restaurant manager. With minor adjustments to titles, the same would be a true statement for any retail business that has front-line employees who deal directly with a customer. To manage across a territory, not only can you not hate the workers to whom you have delegated your entire business plan; you really have to *love* them.

> **"That's the nature of the business we're in— two people interacting inside a one-square-meter imaginary box."**

This doesn't mean you have to be doing a line-level job every time you are in the field, but you have to respect what your people do for you every day. After all, they are the public face of your business and your success is dependent upon their success. I try to point out in seminars that the front-line employees represent the ***magic square meter***, the space between the service provider and the customer where all of the service interaction and revenue exchange occurs during every transaction.

Everything we do in the service business—whether it is serving a hot dog from a cart on the street corner, delivering a pizza to a front door, or pouring a glass of Pinot Noir in a fine dining restaurant—comes down to one service person being less than a meter from a guest, handing him, placing before her, food or drink. That's the nature of business we're in—two people interacting inside a one-square-meter imaginary box.

Fortunately, restaurateurs will always be in this personal service business. There is no way to outsource this function. I cannot serve someone a plate of Lo Mein noodles in Copenhagen from my restaurant in Beijing. It just does not work like an Internet service provider or an online distribution warehouse. We will always need to be within one-square-meter of our customers offering a unique food and service experience.

This being the case, although it might sound obvious it must be emphasized: to be a great *leader of managers* in an operations based company, you have to have an understanding of what people actually do in those operations.

Mastering single-unit operations, when considered as one of the eight key success areas for multi-unit managers, means being responsible for, among other things, cost control, personnel training, and the maintenance of facilities.

These responsibilities are typically considered the sole concern of the single-unit manager. But here we see illustrated the meaning of Peter Drucker's phrase "managing managers." The single-unit manager, no matter how competent she is, needs the multi-unit manager to help her accomplish her goals. Her goals must be his goals, and his goals her goals.

Simply put, the multi-unit manager must know what is being done at each and every unit. No matter if your business is a simple French bakery, a regional Panini/sandwich place, or a coffee shop, you need to understand what your restaurant does that is unique, what makes it different operationally than, say, a fine dining, Northern Italian restaurant. You have to understand what makes your business tick.

Standard Operating Procedures

Multi-unit operations strive to attain maximum productivity, where productivity simply means the relationship between what you put in and what you get out. Our unit productivity is measured by how much value we can derive from every labor dollar invested in our business compared to how much revenue we receive.

Maximizing productivity requires two complementary activities: gathering information, and implementing effective management strategies. When everything in an operation runs on time, when everything meets clearly defined standards, when we create less waste and see less loss from underutilized labor, our productivity increases.

Standard Operating Procedures are what separate the single-unit owner from corporate professionals. SOPs are the difference between a cook in his home kitchen and the cook in a restaurant kitchen. Standardized recipes, of course, but also preventive maintenance manuals, daily checklists, as well as formal policies and procedures—these define our professionalism and help the multi-unit manager maintain control across many individual units.

Multi-Unit Strategic Planning

In most cases, we don't think of unit managers as being responsible for making many *strategic* decisions. We think of them as responsible for *tactical* decisions. By definition, the difference between *strategic* management and *tactical* management is the time frame, or the planning horizon. Most definitions suggest that tactical management decisions are about actions that will be completed within a year's time, while strategic decisions are meant for actions that will take a year or longer to reach completion.

The overwhelming majority of what we do in life is tactical. The strategic decisions we make in a given culture are easily enumerated. In the United States, many of us have to decide on such issues as whether to attend a certain college or enter into military service, when to buy a house (which requires taking on a fifteen to thirty-year mortgage), when to buy a car, or with whom and when to get married. Other than these profound decisions, everything else in life can be seen as pretty much tactical in nature.

The same is true for the restaurant at the unit level. Almost no decision that unit managers have the authority to take will make a difference beyond the next month. Rarely will they need to take into consideration any length of time beyond three months. Accordingly, their planning horizons are typically 30, 60, or 90 days in advance. Given the perception of rapid change in the marketplace, many mid-level multi-unit managers assume they can't predict anything beyond three months in the future.

But to be an effective multi-unit manager requires thinking not just tactically, but also strategically. To be a *leader of managers,* you have to look beyond the end of this year. You have to ask yourself where your business will be next year, or perhaps, in two years. You have to ask yourself how you can apply the knowledge you've gained in the short-term to a longer-term perspective. You now have to see the big picture for five, six or ten units. Therefore it is crucial that you carefully consider those decisions that may not reveal their true effect until six, nine or even 12 months have passed.

This is one of the biggest challenges faced by anyone making the transition from unit manager to multi-unit manager—moving from the present to the future, facing the unknown. As a unit manager it is acceptable to worry about whether you will be fully staffed in two hours when the shift changes. As a multi-unit manager you need to ask yourself whether in nine months all of your units will have a fully trained management team in place that is capable of implementing company goals and capturing more market share than the competition by the end of the fiscal year. This transition—from tactician to strategist—is very, very hard.

It is complicated because most unit managers lead very structured routines in their daily work. We say you "run a restaurant" because, when well maintained, restaurants operate very much like machines. Each day the lights get turned on, the "fire is lit in the box," the walk-in is fully stocked, the staff shows up, and the cash drawer leaves the safe. At the end of the day, it all happens in reverse and the machine is put into "power saver" mode. It has been a successful day for a unit manager if nobody has died, the place didn't catch on fire, and all of the money got deposited in the bank. In this terribly random but highly structured and remarkably predictable world, everything happens at roughly the same time every day; only the customers change (but thankfully not all).

When you become a multi-unit manager, that comfortable structure disappears completely. From the day you take on the new role you are now in control of your own schedule and your own work structure. You decide where you will go, which units you will visit and when, who you need to coach or compliment, and how much time it will require to do it all. For many people it is very hard to transition from the comfortable, structured life of unit management to the insecure, unstructured life of the *leader of managers* where the people needing management might be the same, but the issues they create rarely are.

Interpersonal and Social Responsibilities

The multi-unit manager has to know what's going on outside the walls of her units. She has to know where the business is heading, and why that direction is different than a competitor's. She has to know what gives her business a sense of identity, and she has to know how to control this sense in the eyes of the marketplace.

The multi-unit manager has to know where and how to get the people he needs for the future. If I lose a unit manager next year to family leave, as a multi-unit manager, I have to know who's going to replace him or her. I need to be constantly looking for the best people to go out and hire or to hire from within. And I need to know how the community reacts to what our business is doing. I need to be constantly looking *out the front door*.

Multi-unit managers must be more aware of the entire surrounding community than they ever were in a single unit. This awareness includes everything from finding and developing managers who might be enticed to work for the competition to ensuring customer safety in the public parking lot next door.

Travel and Visiting Units

Everybody knows visiting units is a major portion of a multi-unit manager's job. Sometimes you let people know that you are coming to allow them time to prepare. Sometimes you just have to show up without them knowing. You have to be there, occasionally in the right place at the wrong time. As Ken Blanchard has said, you want to catch people doing things right, but once in a while you also want to catch people doing things wrong.

When I ran restaurants, one of my favorite things to do was to say good-bye to everybody at 8:00 pm, but then about an hour later return to stand outside and watch through the windows. It was like watching a live performance. I was the director of the show on the other side of the "fourth wall." I was seeing a teamwork together successfully but without any direct involvement from me.

Site visits are crucial to successful multi-unit management, and like many activities in a manager's toolbox, both a regular schedule and moderate randomness help to keep everyone on their best behavior. The time spent in a unit is the most important time for the *leader of managers*, because that is when role modeling is best exhibited, talent development is most possible, and daily operations may be best observed.

One of the best *leader of managers* I have known, my friend Doug Doran, insisted that all the MUMs in his division spend a full day and a half on every site visit, which included an overnight stay. The visit started with morning meetings, observation of lunch service, afternoon meetings, observation of dinner service including table visits with guests, and observation of closing procedures. The next day begins with an observation of the opening process and then concludes with an extensive debriefing of the entire unit management team, not only the unit manager. He also insisted that during the structured part of the visit the MUM's cell phone, laptop or tablet be left in a briefcase or the car. Time could only be scheduled for catching up on emails and messages during specific short periods during the visit or off-site.

Doug's program may not be feasible for every company. Nevertheless time must be dedicated to thorough on-site review. Otherwise you end up with threadbare impressions, not the complete picture.

Human Relations

Whenever you as multi-unit manager walk into a unit; whenever you make your site visits, announced or unannounced; every time you talk to a customer or an assistant manager—you represent the company. You might not consider it all the time, but you always represent the desires of every employee in the company. They should want to be you; they should want your job. Even if they don't think about it often, they at times clearly say to themselves, "I admire her; she is an incredible person to work for." That's the definition of role modeling.

On a daily, weekly or monthly basis, the *leader of managers* is modeling company and personal values, whether she is encouraging team building or focusing efforts on quality improvements. Even customers are included in this modeling behavior. They are very much aware of the entire management team and how it interacts during site visits, whether planned or unplanned.

This is all to say, the *leader of managers* must be sure to "take time to be a manager" this means he must concentrate his full attention on the people he is responsible for managing. Management is focused on individual actions; leadership is focused on group behaviors.

Effective Leadership

As a tool to help focus the work of the *leader of managers,* the meaning of "effective leadership" is very specific. We have positioned it to demonstrate the necessity of serving as a resource for all levels of management in the area. Leaders are expected to exhibit a breadth of knowledge, even wisdom, when they mentor and coach younger or less experienced managers. We believe this is especially important when coaching the next generation of assistant unit managers, who make up the "bench-strength" that represents the company's future.

Being an effective leader requires attending to unit managers and aiding them in their efforts to increase sales and customer frequency through staff training and unit development.

Unit Level Finances

The eighth and final factor, which is focused on the management of unit level finances, is positioned almost directly in the center of the four quadrants. As described previously in the text, and as pointed out by everyone from Drucker to Kotter, the primary purpose of a business is to make a profit. Drucker says that profits should be considered like any other expense. They are the "cost of staying in business."

Understanding the complex relationships among the investments in people, operations, planning and profits requires striking a true balance on a daily basis. Making financial decisions with regards to everything from menu pricing to unit-level hiring, from advertising programs to capital improvements, is a real challenge. This key area of success is therefore perfectly balanced along both the **Operations—Strategy** and the **Human Resource Management—Finance** axes.

4

The Individual in Balance

Being Both Manager and Leader

The *leader of managers* will find that her time and focus often shift among three perspectives. And she should discover a balance in her schedule for modeling all three roles which she is required to perform, that of Administrator, Manager and Leader. I will briefly present a definition of each role, but it is important to keep in mind that while still important for success, the functions of the administrator are most easily delegated, and for most people the least challenging to master.

Each part has its own challenges and rewards, and all three are necessary to be successful in her new role. During the course of the *leader of managers'* transition, each multi-unit manager will be called to exhibit the skills of the administrator, the manager and the leader, sometimes all within a few minutes of each other.

Administration occurs when an individual integrates and enforces organizational policies and practices. His activities include collecting, organizing and communicating information while maintaining control over variability and undesirable systemic change. In a short phrase: **Administrators integrate.**

Management happens when an individual implements, maintains or plans for programs, procedures and systems. Her activities are task related and include planning, budgeting and analysis. In summation: **Managers implement.**

Leadership is when an individual inspires people, often to take action they wouldn't take without the leader. His activities include setting goals, sharing a vision for the future, behavior modeling, mentoring and team building. Simply stated: **Leaders inspire.**

She will need to know when the time is right to use each role to accomplish her goals. It is important to remember—even though all three roles are critical to being a successful *leader of managers*—in her daily work life most people are: *unaware of* the work done by the administrator unless it leads to a procedural bottleneck; they *work for* a manager with little loyalty or thought unless there is reason to fear him; but they *follow* a leader, often without concern for other personal rewards or expected returns.

New Perspective and Approaches

In order to become effective and move from acting as a multi-unit manager, the *leader of managers* must utilize as many techniques and skills as she can develop. Since much of a unit level general manager's decision making is based on situational analysis they tend to take a traditional "hands on" approach. As noted earlier, as the *leader of managers* grows and redefines her role, decision-making begins to become more conceptual, with a longer time horizon and therefore more visionary.

Obviously, all levels of management in an organization must be flexible and be able to adapt to each new set of circumstances and challenges as they arise. Each time a situation calls for a decision, a balance may be struck by using the appropriate approach drawn from the experiences a manager has learned to master over time.

One way of seeing this back-and-forth interplay between the perspective of a unit manager and the role assumed by the *leader of managers* is illustrated in the following chart (see **Figure 13**). Rather than presenting an "either/or" decision scenario, this presents the concept of "both/and" choice, and should also be seen as complementary to the three models previously presented.

THE BALANCED *LEADER OF MANAGERS*		
Managerial Approach	**"both/ and"**	*Leadership Approach*
Numbers Focused		*People Focused*
Cost Controlling		*Revenue Enhancing*
Studies Past Information		*Looks Ahead & Plans*
Product Driven		*Market & Brand Driven*
Skills Oriented		*Concept Oriented*
Avoids Conflict (Reactive)		*Uses Conflict (Proactive)*
Responsibility without Authority		*Authority based on Responsibility*
Top-Down Decision Making		*Shared Decision Making*
Intuitive & Experiential		*Analytical & Experimental*
Conventional Wisdom		*Breakthrough Thinking*
Accepting Competitive Standards		*Seeking Competitive Advantage*
Conservative, Risk Avoiding		*Innovative, Risk Assessing*
Labor as a Necessary Expense		*Labor as a Profit-Making Asset*
Asset Supervisor		*Sales, Information & Revenue Manager*

Figure 13

For example, a unit manager must be keenly focused on her period Income Statement, truly being focused on the "numbers." The multi-unit manager needs to continue to keep unit budgeting and profitability in mind, but balances this inward view with a broader focus that looks more at the development of people and how talented individuals use those numbers to advance the business.

The manager studies past weekly, monthly and quarterly operating results, while the leader looks forward to plan operating results for the next quarter, the upcoming six months, or a year in the future. In balance, good managerial decisions need to consider past results to see trends and budget exceptions, good leadership needs to set a clear course for others to follow.

The manager might rely on the efficiency of top-down decision-making, while the leader is more open to the effectiveness of cooperative decision-making and consensus building. In balance, certain situations call for immediate action to be taken by the one in charge, yet delegation and shared decision making develops critical thinking in junior managers.

Evolution of the Manager/Leader Role

How often have we all heard that nothing is certain except for change? Now that restaurant meals have become a crucial part of the global lifestyle, the changes that affect society in general will have significant impact on the multi-unit environment. One such change is the increasing "pluralism of consumer demand," meaning that our guests continually want more choices of better and more differentiated product offerings.

With this has also come a "pluralism of the supply of talent." This means that every day the service labor force becomes more diverse, less and less homogeneous in education, harder to motivate and without a shared cultural knowledge.

The New Operations Manager

The definition of operations excellence is changing with consumers and talent just as quickly. Technology is driving this change, as both big data and miniaturization create new challenges and new competency requirements for the *leader of managers*.

Computers will no longer simply be collectors of information from the POS system they will be used to monitor every activity in the restaurant from employee time cards to "use by dates" for dairy products. Technology is always defined in two realms, hardware— new machines, equipment and utensils; and software--systems, organizations and techniques. Hardware inevitably sells on price as new equipment and machines are introduced.

Software often becomes personalized by the consumer and creates demand for new ways to provide custom services. Systems which allow for local product procurement, organic food sourcing, nutritional composition of all menu items, tracking of individual customer choices, and basic food safety and science will all become part and parcel of the unit manager's daily work load.

"Technologies"

Hardware	Software
Machines	Systems
Equipment	Organization
Utensils	Techniques

The cooking line in a kitchen is hardware driven, as is a basic back bar inventory, and there is little competitive advantage to be gained by either. But when the kitchen features the hot new chef and his signature dish, or the bar has the city's leading mixologist pouring her artisan cocktails, the software drives business.

So, to be promoted to a multi-unit level, all of these skills, and many others, will need to be mastered. The balanced multi-unit manager, in order to keep abreast of social media savvy customers, technophile employees and waves of operations data, will evolve into the *Information Technology Manager* for her system of restaurant units.

Basically, there will be more technological change during the next decade than there has been since Escoffier designed the hierarchical kitchen brigade system at the end of the 19th Century. Companies, and managers themselves, will need to find the means to acquire the education necessary to master all of these factors. Change will indeed require new skills, and the role of the unit manager will change too. The *leader of managers* will be required to master both the hardware and the software of this new technology wave.

The New Facilities Manager

As in so many areas of modern society, managers will need to master layer upon layer of newly emerging physical plant technologies. From a simple labor cost to capital improvements looking to replace labor completely, or from just-in-time purchasing software to cook-chill systems, technology will drive the skills of the unit manager.

For example, within a very short time a significant portion of the cost structure for all businesses will revolve around energy management. Restaurants will need to monitor all manner of energy, waste, and other environmental factors, either because of changing laws and government regulation or pressure from the investment community for cost reductions.

Miniaturization and greening of kitchen equipment through advanced microprocessors is already happening. Where a simple understanding of refrigeration technology used to be a plus for a unit manager, in the very near future she will be required to understand the workings of remote digital wireless sensors, heat pumps, co-generation equipment, and blast chillers just to comply with regulations. The role of the LOM will include being the *Manager of Environmental Engineering* for the restaurants in his district.

The New Finance Manager

As described in this book, managers will also be required to manage their business units by understanding not only a simplified Profit & Loss Statement, but how the total Income Statement drives positive Cash Flows, which in turn creates increasing value on the Balance Sheet. Where this level of financial sophistication used to be reserved mainly for senior executives, competencies in all aspects of the business will soon be expected of general managers in most corporate units.

Just as the unit manager's role and responsibility will continue to change, the role and responsibility of *the leader of managers* to mentor and teach financial skills will also evolve. With a portfolio of six to ten strategic business units, it is not at all unlikely that the LOM will have direct control of more than 250 employees, a combined 25-30 individuals with a "management" title, and annual revenues ranging from 10 to 50 million dollars, greater than many mid-size companies. The LOM will also wear the hat of the *Manager of Finance and Accounting* for his restaurant network.

The New Marketing Manager

A big part of this evolution will come with the need to understand the principles of customer relationship management. This means, for example, having the ability to create, manage, and track local store social media campaigns which are integrated into a total neighborhood marketing program.

Promotional activities, public relations, sales blitzes, and the integration of the community into the daily routines of the enterprise will become a major component of every general manager's job description. Add the rapid rise of customer communication via the Internet, specifically through Facebook, Twitter, LinkedIn, mobile Apps, Yelp, YouTube, or whatever is current in the future and there is an almost uncontrolled level of expertise necessary in a new combined marketing and technology skill set. The LOM will become the de facto *Sales and Marketing Manager* for her operating units.

The New Human Resources Manager

So, how will a balance between manager and leader be created? What will be the new success factors for future unit general managers looking to be promoted to the level of *leader of managers*? Of primary importance is that they will have to become true "generalists" with a strong mastery of organizational complexity and experience managing in a less structured and more insecure market.

These generalists will need to be able to move rapidly from: downloading on-line computer reports to meeting with community activists; from conversing bilingually with staff and customers to creating in-store merchandising campaigns; all while dealing with a more mobile work force who sees their jobs as little more than a temporary stop on the way to somewhere else. To manage this generation of new unit managers, the LOM will need to embrace a new role, becoming the *Manager of Human Capital* for his region.

Here is a thought: a great corporate operations manager (another description of the *leader of managers*) is really a highly paid regional *Human Resource Director* who happens to work in the field. At the end of the week, the most important challenge she has to overcome is finding a way to motivate and retain a team of great people. She is the coach, the mentor, the role model for her entire team, and their success is her success.

5

The Individual in Transition

As the *leader of managers* concepts are assimilated by the evolving multi-unit manager evidence should be found that as an individual he will begin to make noticeable transitions in each of eight areas. He should see himself moving from the successful unit manager to the successful multi-unit manager, and ultimately to a *leader of managers* all within the 24-month timeline proposed earlier.

During this time of transition an LOM should be able to take time for self-analysis and reflection on how far she has progressed in her personal development. A significant part of this will be the challenge of being able to measure her transition along these eight dimensions. Because so much of the work of a multi-unit manager is self-directed and unstructured, it is imperative that she create her own structured environment.

The Eight Areas

In the previous section we talked about finding a balance between manager and leader. Here I am suggesting that the multi-unit manager will show a noticeable and measurable change in perspective as he matures. He will transition from:

Technical Trainer to Management Developer

Training is a necessity in any business environment where skills are repeated, and processes can be standardized. Activities such as following a recipe, making a wine suggestion, or learning how to seat parties professionally are each trainable skills. These and the many other tasks of team members in the kitchen, dining room or bar lend themselves ideally to training protocols.

On the other hand, devising and implementing an individual management development plan for each assistant manager in a 10 unit district requires taking into account their individual existing strengths, weaknesses and needs. Creating carefully written plans with benchmarks at 30, 60 and 90 days for an entire team is one measure of this transition.

Information Receiver to Information Communicator

The transitioning MUM realizes that business information is neither a one way flow (from unit to district) nor meant to be kept tightly controlled (there are few "top secret" messages in restaurant management). To perform well, individuals need relevant information from their boss, and the boss needs actionable information from them.

The evolving manager learns that he needs to have regularly scheduled, but meaningful, face to face meetings with his management team, and uses well timed social media and electronic communication tools such as Twitter and emails to set clear goals through voice messages and texts. Simplistically, the unit manager collects data and sends it to the "home office" then waits for it to bounce back. The multi-unit manager repackages it and sends it up further in the chain, still waiting for a response.

The transitioning *leader of managers* analyzes information, gives it meaning, and shares it with the people who need to use it, both up at corporate, but more importantly back in the unit where the information is useful for success tomorrow.

A Structured Work Environment to an Unstructured Work Environment

The manager of a single restaurant unit is guided by the seasonality of the customer. Breakfast, lunch and dinner are always served around the same time, Friday night is typically busier than Wednesday night, and Monday morning is usually the start of the business week. The rhythm of the day, week, month or season is matched by the work schedule of the unit manager.

But promotion into area management and out of that comfortable rhythm of the unit brings a challenge. Now the schedule is determined by the MUM herself. Should she make a surprise visit to the underperforming older store, or spend a few minutes with the young team at the just opened restaurant on the other side of town? Should she take her car, the train, or walk to her appointments, or simply spend the morning in the home office catching up on administrative paperwork? The externally defined structure that was so comforting as a general manager is gone and has been replaced by a completely self-guided and self-defined day on her own.

"Doer" to "Delegator"

I was told many years ago by Larry Owens, a medium size quick-service franchise operator, that he had two kinds of multi-unit managers. There were the ones who did lots of things by themselves but didn't care much about "the why" of what they were doing. Then there were the ones who got lots of things done by planning the work and asking others to do things for them.

The first group, what we called the "Super Operator" in early chapters, puts his head down and pushes forward. He knows that the only way to get something done right is to do it himself. The Delegator on the other hand, has made training a priority so that when she asks people to do a task, instructions come with the knowledge, skills and behaviors necessary to get the job done right the first time. She knows that delegation not only makes her more productive, but it is a training tool for the growth and development of all of the people she involves in her projects.

This is part of the practice that my friend Joe Hayes and I call, "Ask, Suggest, Teach." When presented with a problem by a subordinate, the LOM will ask that assistant or general manager what three remedies they might suggest be considered. From those three suggestions will spring a "teachable" moment, so that after discussion about the outcomes each one presents, together they will decide on a course of action. That action, in turn, is delegated to the subordinate, with the outcome reviewed later. Managers will begin to internalize the process and make better suggestions often without further consultation. Ultimately, comfortable on their own, the process leads to better decision-making at the unit level, and a more productive *leader of managers*.

People Influencing Activities to Team Motivating Techniques

As noted in standard management texts, the manager often has very little choice in how to get things done at the individual employee level. There is the carrot and stick, the promise of future reward, or perhaps creating the desire not to be embarrassed in front of coworkers and friends. The savvy manager realizes that persuasion is the art of getting things done through other people. But in each of these cases, the manager is attempting to influence the actions of an individual employee. Out of necessity the unit manager, who works where much of the tasks are actually completed, either becomes a master at this art or does not survive.

The LOM brings that individual people influencing skill with him to the new role, but must also quickly make the transition into motivating large numbers of employees to act together for a single goal. He is no longer afforded the privilege of simply taking action through charisma, personal charm or even fear, but must move an entire team through role modeling and setting clear visions for the future.

A Paternalistic "One Boss" Environment to an Inclusive and Peer Interdependent "Team Managed" Environment

Many people remember the days of "my way or the highway" in the full-service restaurant business. The manager/owner was in complete control, a self-styled king and no one dared to cross him, or he was the benevolent despot doling out favors to his loyal subjects.

In the early days of the Quick-Service segment, in companies from McDonald's to Taco Bell, there were people with, or nearly similar to, the title Franchise Development Specialist. They typically had responsibilities for three to five independent franchisee units, often supervising through fear and intimidation. The real fear came from threats that units not meeting inspection standards could be stripped from the current operator at a moment's notice. A kind term for them was the "franchise gorillas," who would conduct surprise inspections and as the name implied, use the time to pound their chests, bellowing and making noise while everyone cowered in a corner until they left. While those days are mostly gone, the remnants sometime remain.

The strong-willed or self-centered super star unit manager, upon promotion to multi-unit management may, as noted, fall quickly into the trap of "one boss" and its traditional command and control decision-making with little perceived personal risk. Today the true *leader of managers* transitions past this top down and paternalistic style, seeking instead to manage people in a team-centered and certainly more respectful partnership style of approach.

Reliance on Old Skills to Building New Business Knowledge and Behaviors

When we described the "5 Phases Model" we defined the Super Operator as someone pretty much stuck in place. Here I refer specifically to the person who is capable, and willing, to move past the comfort level of his old skills and embrace new business models.

Later, in Section 4 we will look at how people view change and how important it is for a growing company. The *leader of managers* must be a catalyst for change, with his personal change being measured in terms of the acceptance of new business concepts and products, new management structures and activities, or new processes for leadership using new systems.

Asset Supervisor to Asset Enhancer

Finally, a significant transition in the way an "operator" sees her role in the enterprise must occur. I only half-heartedly joke that a successful unit manager is the person who: opens a restaurant early in the morning; turns on the "factory/machine" by igniting the fire-in-the-box in the kitchen; checks to make sure there will be enough staff, food and beverages to get through the day; places the cash drawer in the register; and then watches the customers through lunch and dinner to make sure as many leave standing up as came walking in.

At the end of the day, the reverse is the rule: put the food back in the walk-in and the staff on the street; turn off the fire-in-the-box; take the cash and lock it in the safe; and check to make sure no patron is hiding in the

> **"Take away my people, but leave my factories, and soon grass will grow on the factory floors. Take away my factories, but leave my people, and soon we will have a new and better factory."**
>
> **Andrew Carnegie**

bathroom before locking the door. The "operator" has just three real measures of success each day: no one died, the place didn't burn down, and the money got into the safe. This is the definition of an asset supervisor. The building and its contents were kept intact; there was no loss in value, but not much gain either.

The transformation to Asset Enhancer happens when the *leader of managers*, through his decisions, vision and inspirational leadership encourages unit managers and their teams to go beyond the simple daily operational routine. The LOM creates systems and practices which add value to the enterprise, making the physical asset worth more at the end of the day, week, month or season than it was when they began to lead.

She accomplishes this by showing evidence of long-term planning and investing in the future of the business, especially focusing on the development of her people.

Managing in Four Directions

Almost everyone understands that we are expected to manage the people below us on the organization chart. In reality the LOM actually manages in four directions. This management challenge includes: his obvious direct reports, but also his bosses, and individuals in both lateral directions like his peers in the organization and others over whom he has no direct control.

Managing in Four Directions

In any multi-unit organization, there will be both cooperation and competition among the many unit managers and their teams. Each unit manager, by the nature of the business, will be vying for attention from the LOM, even while they are all trying to avoid being directly controlled.

What is not always understood, though, is that we manage in the other three directions, as well. You might have heard it said that we need to "manage up" to get what we want. This is very true; the LOM will need to make sure that his goals and the goals of his superiors are in alignment so that his decisions and his actions not only reflect well on him, but on the people who he reports to and those who report to him.

Additionally, on occasion she will need to manage some people over whom she has almost no direct control. Customers basically fall into the category of "uncontrolled others," they need to be managed so that the LOM can attain her sales and profitability goals. Unfortunately, patrons have their own needs and desires, remember, ultimately it's the customers who are the ones making the decision on what gets sold, how much gets sold, and whether she had accurately forecasted their behaviors. To meet sales projections and both labor and food costs, the customers have to be managed. At the end of the day, have her decisions meant that her restaurants have met consumer desires, so they dine there more often and think of her restaurants before they consider any other restaurant company?

Personal Growth and People Development

As part of the LOM's personal development plan there is the requirement that he focus his attention on the specific individual needs of the team he leads.

Marcus Buckingham believes that the "best managers spend 80% of their time trying to amplify their people's strengths." The human resource consulting firm, Hewitt Associates, has found that "the best companies grow their talent in-house." A significant part of her job as a *leader of managers* is to identify the strengths, weaknesses and opportunities for advancement that are both needed by and shown by her area team members.

Obviously, not everyone works in the same manner. The LOM needs to customize his management style to fit both his needs and the individual needs of his team members. One suggestion is to create a **"Key Personnel Inventory"** for the 10, 20 or 30 managers/supervisors in his area. Items to include might be an assessment of each manager's work style (intense, playful, loose/tight), personality traits (humorous, serious, thoughtful, aggressive), or job history (line cook, server, retail floor, cashier, other company employment). It is up to him to create, design and then integrate this kind of management tool into his daily work life.

For example, what many senior managers find helpful when they are accountable for a large number of subordinates, as she will be, is to identify one or two "touchstones" for each direct report she has. These items are unique to each person, and help to trigger her memory about a person's entire personality. In order for her to create a unique personal development program for everyone, she needs to know each person's particular strengths and needs. From this inventory of attributes she can begin to craft a meaningful long term "goals and aspirations" plan for each manager in her area.

Additionally, as he develops a personal relationship with each management team member, he will also start to create a plan for personal accountability—both for himself and the members of his team. As many have said before, *"What you measure is what you get."* The goal is to build a stronger team of high performance individual stars. What he needs to measure is how well he, as an individual *leader of managers,* has helped others develop and change.

Tracking Management DNA

Proof of individuals making the transition from trainer to developer can be tracked company-wide, with the added benefit of revealing the existence of a clear path of cross-generational company DNA being transferred from one manager to another. At the time each candidate is being groomed for promotion, she should be asked about the people who have influenced her success. There should be a system in place for identifying which managers in the company she has worked with so she could reach this level of promotion. These people, the managers who have been most influential as people developers, are a true company resource. They will all have different traits and characteristics, but like the DNA in a family, they will all carry core identifiers inside them. Great companies find that DNA and capitalize on it.

As management writer Jay Conger suggests a company should "track the performance of the people who a manager promotes." It is by their success that his will be measured. How has he created individualized development programs for his area team members as he transitioned to a developer mindset?

A similar question can be asked about each of the other seven areas for her transition. Obviously, she will need to make note of, and support, her observations about her own personal development. She should be self-critical, objective about her accomplishments and thoughtful in her assessment of her success.

> **"What you need to measure is how well you as an individual *leader of managers* have helped others develop and change."**

Part Three

THE ORGANIZATION

The Growing Organization

"The Entrepreneur always searches for change, responds to it, and exploits it as an opportunity." Peter Drucker

"In sharp contrast with the income substitutes are the entrepreneurs. They know from the start that they are trying to build a significant corporation....Income appears not to be their primary motivation. They are driven by a desire to create an innovative force in the corporate world." David Birch

The Challenges of Growth and Development for Multi-Unit Company Leaders

Multi-unit restaurant management is all about managing and organizing for growth. Chain restaurants are by their nature growing organizations, in keeping with the MIT management researcher David Birch's definition of an entrepreneurially focused company. Successful companies are the ones who manage their growth, while the highways and street corners are littered with companies that have not.

What is the difference between being a small business and an entrepreneurial multi-unit business? Birch suggested the first should be defined as an enterprise which is providing someone with self-employment or "income substitution." Peter Drucker the great management philosopher said, "The entrepreneur always searches for change, responds to it, and exploits it as an opportunity."

I suggest the differences between a single-unit and a multi-unit enterprise can be plainly seen in five key areas of management focus: Size; Culture; Power & Control; Branding and Lifecycle. Each of these five practices is completely interdependent of the others so that as a company grows from one unit to many units the change in Size requires a change in both Power & Control and company Culture. Or similarly a movement along the Lifecycle curve demands a new approach to a corresponding maturing Brand position.

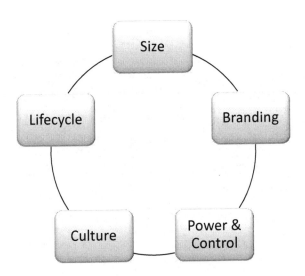

What must be considered in each of these areas is that increasing organizational complexity creates challenges for senior management that would not be present in a smaller single-unit enterprise, even one that has multiple operational functions or numerous strategic business units.

Growing and managing a multi-unit organization is not unusual in today's retail marketplace. In fact, simple applied Microeconomics would suggest it is inevitable given the challenges facing traditional mom-and-pop retailers but success is not a stepwise organic path from one unit to many.

So which of the five key areas comes first? Perhaps growing brand acceptance in the marketplace leads to more units being open to match increasing consumer demand? Or is it that an entrepreneurially focused company culture of "growing at all costs" leads to stronger brand awareness? Maybe the trigger is that as more units are rapidly opened the expansion creates the need for a different system of power sharing and new control mechanisms?

Does the stage along the lifecycle of a company dictate the need for a new emphasis on surfacing cultural normative behaviors, or does the number of units define the place in a company lifecycle? More to the point for the discussion of the challenging role of the *leader of managers*, why are these interdependencies so crucial to success?

1

Size

I have often heard operators say that, "Going from one unit to two was the hardest thing I ever did." But I have just as often heard an entrepreneur say, "Expanding from seven to eight was so much harder than opening my second." And, yes, I have heard the same thing in a slightly different way, "The first twenty-five were tough, but then it became really complicated."

As far back as 1962 the researchers Blau and Scott wrote about the constraints that increasing size present to an organization. Specifically they suggested that as more people work in a company three major issues will appear: increasing need for *formalization and bureaucracy*; a rise in *organizational complexity*; and the challenge of maintaining consistent and *clear communications* across the growing organizational structure.

> "Going from one unit to two was the hardest thing I ever did."

Formalization and Bureaucracy

In the first case, instead of using the now often disparaged term bureaucracy to mean the worst parts of any organizational structure, they were referring to the positive organizing concept originally offered by Max Weber. In the 1930's Weber said that for organizations to move from simple to complex there will be a corresponding change from reliance on a single individual person or personality (who might simply have been promoted into a job or role) to a more formal structure where the position someone has is defined by the set of skills necessary for the work they need to master. His theory was meant to show how the organization of workers into a formal structure would add to productivity and efficiency, not make it worse.

> "The first twenty-five were tough, but then it became really complicated"

Literally, the bureau is the physical office and/or the title that a manager is occupying, for example the Director of Marketing or the Vice-President of Operations. It makes sense that as a company expands, and adds new employees, that a new organizational structure will need to be put in place to match this expansion. If every employee added to the organization was just simply hired without some corresponding increase in management oversight, it is easy to imagine that true chaos would soon follow.

So Weber used the word bureau to mean both an office, as in the physical place where a clerk, supervisor or manager might work, and the job skills that would be assigned to the work done in that place. A bureaucracy is simply a collection of the offices that senior managers in an organization have created in which to assign specific work to a variety of specific professionals.

For example, in an independent or small franchise start-up company the founder of the company will naturally be loyal to his opening crew. As more units are added, his first employee, "Tom" might be promoted to Area Manager because he has shown loyalty and promise as the company's first unit manager. But Tom might be filling one, two or more other more informal positions, with efficiency sacrificed for immediacy. In this situation in addition to operations, Tom may also be in charge of all local marketing, perhaps making sales calls to the business community in the area on an *ad hoc* or project-by-project basis.

As formalization in the organization increases there will come a time when instead of making an offer to the original team member Tom, outsider Rachel should be hired because she exhibits the qualifications that match the new position (even if that means Tom is bypassed for a promotion until his personal development plan is complete).

Entrepreneurial companies typically take advantage of their available resources, especially their human resources, by being expedient and finding the best available person to "fit" the immediate needs, but they may not be finding the best "actual" person for the job. A larger company on the other hand will actively seek someone with the skills necessary for the "office." A formal bureaucracy has been formed. As the company continues to grow, the job of, say, Director of Marketing and Sales will become clearly defined with a job description and clear expectations. Whereas in the past the founder of a small company may look at the existing team and ask someone who has an interest in that particular area to take the job, now competency not seniority will be the deciding factor.

The constraint in this case is that a growing organization may not see the building of formal infrastructure as a core competency but rather as an obstacle to success. The evolving bureaucracy is viewed as a cost, in terms of both actual cash investment and time commitment, something which takes away from the operations objectives of new unit growth and revenue enhancement. Bureaucracy creates a dilemma, especially if it is not disciplined, because it can be perceived as leading to an explosion of "red tape" and the sense that unit management control is being replaced by the burgeoning head office staff.

Organizational Complexity

When more units are added to a growing company portfolio it is obvious that the organization will become more complex. As shown in **Figure 14** with every unit added so are people; it is the people who make an organization more complex. Keep in mind that when this bureaucracy becomes established, many good things will begin to happen as well. Tasks are assigned to the right people, who happen to have the right skills needed to accomplish them. Efficiency goes up and often so does productivity. In order to make this process efficient, tasks must be delegated with more people working on each project. Where once there were just a handful of people involved in all of the excitement and operational decision-making, with each new unit there will be new teams with new ideas.

Unfortunately, as more people take on the completion of each task, the network of relationships at each level also increases. Before, in a smaller company only one or two people were dealing with each issue; the decisions necessary for the completion of a task were made by very few people. Now the

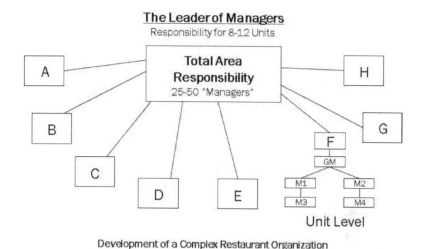

Figure 14

responsibility for decision-making is spread across a number of individuals, or across departments, or across layers of accountability.

As an organization expands it also begins to become much more complex. At some point a formal hierarchy must occur. More workers require more bosses, just as more bosses means more subordinates, who also have subordinates, who are now responsible for making decisions themselves. Letting each of these new layers know what is considered to be the correct company policy can be a daunting challenge.

The overarching concept here is the need to determine an optimal management "span of control" to systemize and simplify the complexity. Span of Control is a management concept identified almost one hundred years ago by Henri Fayol. Basically the number of people for which a manager or supervisor is responsible will determine how an organization is structured, makes collective decisions, and communicates information in both the long- and short-term.

This question, how many people or strategic business units in the organizational structure one manager can efficiently control, has been a topic of debate for generations. Military organizations have used this organizing principle of control since at least the time of the Roman Legions. In the Art of War, Sun Tzu said, "Generally, management of many is the same as management of a few. It is a matter of organization."

Each layer that is added to the organizational hierarchy stretches or contracts management span of control, with Drucker saying the width of any specific span is often related to the level of technological expertise or professional competence of the subordinates who need to be managed. In the multi-unit environment we need to add other variables such as distance or travel time between units, revenue- and profit-generating levels per unit, and competitive market structure to the traditional model. Since by definition all managers must have at least one person to supervise (but may have five, ten, twenty or more direct reports or even operating units) this span of control concept truly applies to all complex organizations.

There are basically two methods for expanding the management of an organization, either you add layers vertically (termed scalar) or departments horizontally (termed functional). If you use the vertical option you are increasing the length of the chain of command by adding multiple levels of management between the units and the top. This can offer efficiencies because the span of control remains narrow with few direct subordinates for each senior manager. But it can also have a negative impact on the reaction time for decision-making as communication channels become longer and slower and decisions need to be "bumped up" the chain of command for approval or down for implementation.

The opposite is true of a horizontal growth option. In this case the span of control becomes very wide and flat, with many departments or units having direct access to senior management. This can be efficient if it is based on a strong centralized control system. Unit managers have direct reporting access to an entrepreneurial founder or other senior manager with no need to filter decision-making through middle management layers in the organization. But as an organization continues to grow and the number of direct reports for a senior manager reaches seven, eight or more individuals, managerial efficiencies can begin to decline from dispersion of focus or a loss of clear authority. In both growth plans, maintaining clear lines of effective communication to subordinates becomes a significant issue.

Communication Challenges

The challenge, of course, is that where there used to be a simple system for the communicating of decisions—basically the boss told everyone else what she wanted—as an organization becomes larger, messages must be communicated through and across all of the new layers, whether up and down or from end to end. This is not unlike the game called "telephone" that children love to play. Start a line of 20 or so young children and tell the first one a short phrase which must be repeated in a low whisper to the next person and so on to the entire group. At the end of the line, the original message is rarely identifiable.

Think how much challenge a growing organization has when it evolves. It goes from being a company where everyone is together at all times getting immediate feedback to one where the founder/entrepreneur is at a headquarters building in a different part of town (or even a completely different time zone) surrounded by a team of middle managers whose job it is to make decisions for her.

One common phrase heard in growing companies is "It's not like it used to be, I just don't know what's going on anymore." This lament in growing organizations is really a signal that the constraints of size are being felt openly. Growth, while happening, is not being satisfactorily managed or completely planned for.

The Four Dilemmas as Size Increases

The same authors mentioned above, Blau & Scott, also suggested that as an organization grows it faces four potential problem areas, which if left unsolved, become considerable obstacles to continued successful expansion. These four dilemmas are: coordination and communications; bureaucratic discipline; professional expertise; and managerial planning & initiative. Each dilemma presents itself as the constraints above become more obvious with increasing organizational size.

Coordination & Communications

Rapidly growing companies need to build infrastructure. Just as growing towns need to build roads so people can efficiently move from one place to another they also need systems of control including coordination of stop signs or traffic lights. Likewise organizations need to build control systems so that information and shared knowledge may move from one operating unit or from one office to another.

The traditional means for this kind of coordination would have been creating operations manuals and specialized training programs. These documents, which institutionalize the rules and regulations considered to be crucial to the workings of the enterprise, become the main means of informing new and existing employees of "how we do things here." In today's technology dependent environment this information infrastructure now requires a mix of face-to-face knowledge transfer as well as computer-to-computer or social media communications systems.

Senior management must include the cost of coordination and communication into the budget process as expansion is considered. Finding the proper way to communicate the needs, desires, and practices of the rapidly expanding organization with the various people who are intended to implement them presents managers with a significant challenge.

Bureaucratic Discipline

Growing organizations expand by creating new organizational infrastructure; basically they grow by having more people doing more things in a structured way. The challenge is that as this infrastructure grows it needs to be managed; this is the domain of organizational design and development. Without well-formed planning unrestrained growth will more times than not lead to rising costs (in both time and money) that often cannot be contained or controlled.

Cash and human resources are stretched thin during expansion which invariably leads to muddling otherwise clear lines of responsibility and authority. It is not uncommon at this stage to hear people in the headquarters or in the field saying about each other, "Whose job is it to…?" All of this may lead to individuals who engage in "turf wars" or "empire building" within the organization. Even in highly successful organizations resource allocations may not benefit from diluted management self-control and a loss of consistent strategic vision.

The dilemma is that both strategic and tactical choices need to be made. Should the company grow new units rapidly and build the supporting infrastructure later or do they invest in infrastructure now to support an organization that is not large or profitable enough to cover increasing expenses? This effectively means that insuring bureaucratic discipline during times of growth requires that all units, departments, divisions and regions stay focused and are well managed as they are added or expanded.

> **"As organizations grow, the 'best and brightest' talent will get called upon to take on more and more tasks."**

Professional Expertise

As organizations grow, the "best and the brightest" talent will get called upon to take on more and more tasks. This is especially true in the small entrepreneurial company that is growing rapidly at its early stages. Someone who has a talent in operations might be called upon to take over a human resources function, for example creating training programs for all newly hired employees.

This person has become highly skilled in one area and has demonstrated a strong commitment to the company. Unfortunately, even though he is well meaning, he probably will not be as competent in a completely different area of need. While it might seem beneficial to satisfy new critical organizational demands with talent from within the company, what happens instead is that the level of expertise actually declines. Not only are the skills in the new area not as good as they might require, but the skill set that the individual manager possessed from her original area of expertise is also diminished because she is no longer devoting any of her time to it. The organization is actually "less smart" than it was before the switch was made.

This transfer of talent is also seen as more and more units in the field are opened. The most successful operating managers, those who might have stayed in older or maturing unit positions where they have established habits and business relationships are instead moved to the newest units as a reward for their service. The "new and improved" stores are very appealing in a growth company for their excitement and income potential from higher unit sales.

A second drain of talent from the units occurs as central corporate positions become developed and internal promotions are offered. When a headquarters office is formed, usually in support of the founder, it is not uncommon for the top performing people (or at least the most loyal and longest serving) to leave the units or field positions they have mastered and to move to take corporate roles in the central office.

This action is sometimes called a "brain drain" because the experienced holders of the institutional knowledge and shared memory move to the headquarters from the street. This distance from the actual retail customer, and the change in organizational culture which it creates, can significantly weaken the entire system and even accelerate the other challenges of complexity and communication we have discussed.

Managerial Planning & Initiative

Finally, as the company grows and face-to-face communication channels become strained, so do the opportunities, rewards, and recognition for initiating new ideas. Complexity takes its toll on individual innovation if there is a perception that ownership of new ideas is shared with those who are not part of a focused team.

"Growth is an Outcome, not a Strategy"

A small company might have a hard-core group of individuals surrounding an entrepreneurial founder or founders who are responsible for doing all of the tactical and strategic planning or new idea generation. As the company grows the decision-making responsibilities becomes more complex and must be delegated outward and downward to a wider and wider team. De-centralization of decision-making is a requirement of growth, but it does come at a certain cost of lower motivation or declining *esprit de corps*.

2

Branding

Over the past four decades, in a slow but inexorable manner, a growing corporate imperative has replaced the independent restaurant and most similar smaller retail enterprises. The business of multi-unit corporate restaurants is as different from that of the single independent restaurant as the daily activities of a 1000-room Hilton Hotel are from a six-room Bed & Breakfast inn. In this new world the owner's reputation is only one part of the value equation. Instead of the owner's name, the business brand name becomes the focus of consumer knowledge and loyalty.

The end of this world has already happened; most people just didn't take the time to notice. The world in question is that of the independent ("owner operator") restaurateur. Their world, driven by decisions of menu, food cost and staffing, has traditionally been centered in the kitchen. This is a **product-centric** enterprise.

The name, talents and reputation of the owner create the value of the "good will" in the restaurant. Picture the romanticized image of the chef patron wandering through the open market at the crack of dawn, haggling over the freshness of the morels and sea bass, in search of items for tonight's perfect *menu degustation*. She will return to her kitchen to 'create' the evening's menu and offer it in very limited quantities. The local products and the chef who personally transforms them into a new entity create the value-added experience in this world.

In doing so, the chef acts like any traditional craftsman. Often the strength (or weakness) of his reputation is revealed only when the owner/operator looks to sell his assets at the end of a career. It is at the sale when restaurant owners discover they have little equity value to show for a life of hard work. Primarily this is because their commitment to daily personal involvement in every aspect of the business does not come with the transfer of the physical property to new owners. The collection of pots, pans, tables and chairs is not what makes the independent restaurant valuable—the perspiration, tears and toil of the owner are. It is not unusual (in fact most people would probably say it is desirable) that every customer in the restaurant is known well by this owner. Contrast this vision with that of a brand name chain restaurant. It would be the rare customer who knew the local owner of a Morton's Steak House or Outback, Panera Bread or Pizza Hut.

Enhancement of the restaurant brand name becomes the benchmark for the operator's daily agenda. This world, driven by decisions of competitive positioning, customer loyalty, frequency of purchase, and top-line revenues is centered in the consumer's living room.

This is a **market-centric** enterprise. The brand name, plus the mix of products, advertising, prices and service creates a promise to the customer that is built on a more complex equation than any independent can offer. Compared to the scene described above, the licensed or franchised restaurant business owner can easily liquidate their good will because it is protected by a strong brand identity. The logos, operating system, trademarks and restaurant trade dress of his unit all represent the value that can be harvested at the time of the sale of this restaurant.

In this section we will address three questions: 1) What is restaurant branding, 2) Why is it important for today's multi-unit operator, and 3) How can it be used as a driving concept in developing the multi-unit enterprise?

The Brand Pyramid

The restaurant brand is comprised of three key component offerings. A restaurant, in order to meet the needs of the market's

The Restaurant Brand

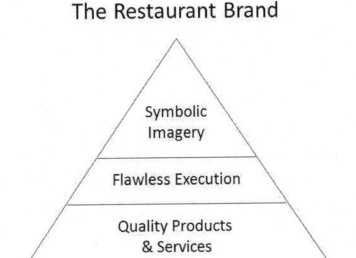

very savvy consumer, must create, present and manage a complete set of these offerings. The restaurant must provide: 1) Quality Products and Services; 2) Flawless Execution of all Service Delivery Systems; and 3) an Established Symbolic and Evocative Brand Image. These three elements must be mastered to meet the competition in today's highly competitive market environment.

The first of these items is the provision of quality products and services. A restaurant product has a distinct set of consumer desirable attributes, such as: items taste better; items are offered in a better portion size for the target market; items are less costly to purchase; or items are easier and more convenient to purchase than those of the competition. A restaurant product also has an identifiable set of characteristics: there is a look to its décor; the menu is designed in a unique way; or the staff presents a certain service profile to the customer. Typically, a product is something that is perceived by the user to have been "made in a factory."

This product regularly has a manufactured, commodity, or mass-produced feel to it. A product is an item which is either durable, it will last for a long period of time, or it is consumable, meaning it is intended to be used up quickly by the purchaser. For example, a simple cup of espresso in a restaurant is nothing more than a product. When it carries an identifying name, say a Cappuccino, it is generically still a product, but when you purchase it in a Starbucks, it has become a branded item.

The concept of "quality products and services" in the restaurant environment means that the above attributes and characteristics are perceived by the consumer as having high value in relation to their purchase cost. In economic terms, they are willing to sacrifice something (its cost to them—the price) in order to maximize their utility of the purchase experience (the benefit they gain by the purchase). Quality is directly related to the price position chosen by the restaurant chain, so McDonald's can offer quality at a relatively low price, but so can T.G.I.Friday's at a higher one. No restaurant chain can compete over the long term if it does not first have products and services which can be delivered over a set of multiple outlets in a consistent and quality manner.

The service delivery requirement means that the chain restaurant organization must seek to provide a guarantee of flawless execution of its operating standards throughout the system. Today's consumer is simply too aware of the difference between good and bad service, and there are too many alternative choices, to settle for anything less than flawless performance by a restaurant company. Simply put, substandard operations will not see patrons return for multiple purchase visits. In the new environment, restaurant enterprise success is measured by increasing frequency of visits, and/or increasing top line revenues. Companies that consistently manage execution, such as Panera Bread or Olive Garden, see their customer frequencies and top-line revenues increasing every year. Both measures are reflective of a flawless operating system.

These two components, quality products and services and flawless execution make up the structural foundation of the restaurant brand offering, success cannot occur without them. They are the outputs of great restaurant organizations. It is in this manner which the most renowned U.S. companies such as McDonald's or Darden Restaurants raise the best practices standard for everyone else to follow.

In contrast to the concept of a product is that of a brand. To complete the third leg of the component relationship requires the establishment of symbolic imagery. A brand is differentiated from other competitive products when it is able to create a unique position in the consumers' mind. Rather than the simple attributes described above, the brand establishes itself as an image, one that has a relationship to other similar or complimentary offerings. Outback Steakhouses are distinctly unique and although originating in the US, the brand evokes an image of Australia as it might be viewed through the eyes of an American consumer. It doesn't matter whether the brand is real, as long as it appears to be authentic and true within its story.

A brand has meaning, not merely characteristics; it is resident in the mind of the targeted purchaser, not made in a factory. Instead of being consumed, it is retained as an image, and once absorbed, can be recalled and reevaluated in relation to other purchases. This imagery is a fusion of the experiences created by the previous two foundation components and is linked to a visual representation through the use of graphic design items such as a logo, advertising copy, registered trademarks and unit level trade dress. A cup of espresso served in a paper cup with a Starbucks logo by a trained barista is worth considerably more than at another coffee shop because it is the beneficiary of the power the company's brand name has to evoke an image in the consumer's mind for quality.

Restaurant Brands for a Changing Landscape

Changes in markets create entrepreneurial seams of opportunities. Market unity is creating opportunities for multi-unit restaurant companies to expand their brand offerings like no time in the past. This unity brings with it many of the advantages that companies have had in North American markets for almost half a century of restaurant company development. As an example, using McDonald's traditional market estimate of one restaurant for every 25,000 people in a relevant trade area, the European Union could support over 14,000 Golden Arched restaurants. The EU, if it followed a similar path for development as the recent US market, could easily support one million total restaurants, of which over 450,000 would be branded chain retail outlets.

A brand makes a promise to the consumer—"you may trust me again and again." This trust has at least three positive aspects. It lowers the purchase cost associated with searching for an alternative product with similar or more desirable attributes, it increases the sense of the familiar thereby lowering consumer insecurity, and it rewards the 'right' consumer behavior by guaranteeing a 'no mistakes' purchase each and every time.

Applying the Brand Building Principles

Every restaurant enterprise has the potential to establish itself as a brand name in the consumer's mind. To do this, brand managers must be aware of the steps that are necessary for building the 'brand organization.'

If we use this idea, the ideal mix of products and services must be offered which will capture the greatest number of customers. While a menu with many items might appear to make a restaurant more attractive to families who simply cannot decide what to have for dinner, it can be argued that a limited menu would do just as well for a different target group. Cheesecake Factory has an extensive food and beverage mix and appeals to a very broad customer base. Longhorn Steakhouse focuses primarily on steaks, a menu which appeals to a narrower, but carefully targeted customer base. Both US companies are expanding into international markets because both have identified the products and services that their targeted customers desire.

Once the proper product mix has been calculated and established, markets must be identified and then optimized to reach a group of likely consumers. For example, as a restaurant concept, the UK's dominant mid-service concept Pizza Express needs to be situated in high foot-fall, up-market locales for its stylish, yet casual, full-service fresh made pizza menu. Given the requirement of its primarily dine-in model and more upscale ingredients at a higher average ticket price, a small suburban bedroom community may not satisfy the core threshold demands to reach break-even. Joey's, a pizza delivery company in Germany, on the other hand can thrive in a small or otherwise undesirable location because most of its pizza sales come from off-site customers and the brand can be developed through consistent delivery execution and quality ingredients.

When the market has been clearly defined, the resources to build the brand company must be accumulated. These resources are not limited to the logistics of acquiring cost-effective food and beverages. It is also a necessity that a supply of qualified management, service and culinary staff be readily available. The development of a brand position through the creation of symbolic imagery is also a resource-based advertising requirement.

Resources are needed for the acquisition of the organizational tools, management skills and creative personnel who have the ability to build a restaurant brand in the target market segment.

Without the resources to produce and reach them, products and markets only represent unfulfilled potential. As these resources are acquired, the next key component is the marshaling of management resources into the establishment of a company, the brand organization, which is market focused and consumer responsive. This company must be customer driven if it is to build a simple restaurant offering into a brand. The restaurant enterprise becomes organized around the attributes and practices that enhance relationships to loyal customers as well as to those patrons who are the highest contributors to the company's profitability.

As this happens, markets become developed by carefully building the organization to respond to specific target customer needs. The brand organization communicates its core values and a vision to both the outside environment and the internal workforce. This organization is directed and led by a team of managers whose job it is to create these lines of communication. What the brand stands for, what meaning it has for its target customer, how the brands 'personality' is different than the competition, all of these things are designed and carefully maintained by an effective brand management team.

Finally, the newly developed brand must have as its backbone a distinctive corporate culture. Top management, in developing the other key components, guides the integration of the brand image and symbolic meaning, the value-driven organization, and the loyal users of the brand, into the creation of a new community, with its own history and cultural norms. The restaurant brand organization has a history and a life which is distinct and different than any single story of its many units or component parts.

The market for restaurants has changed; even a casual observer can tell that this is true. This market continues to develop into a more complex model with every passing day. The older skills of restaurant management—craft based culinary competence and local community knowledge—will not be enough to succeed in the future. Restaurant companies, with sophisticated managers who have mastered the business and economic skills of retail brand building will make it successively harder for the independent operator to compete with also acquiring those skills. It is through the aggressive application of new techniques and principles which will allow the next generation of restaurant companies to thrive.

3

Power and Control

Organizational theorists tell us that when an individual joins an organization, whether they are paid or volunteer, whether the position is professional or amateur, or whether the organization is profit driven or not for profit, there is a tacit understanding that some rules, normative behaviors, or structure exists which will govern the interaction between that individual and the organization itself. For commercial organizations, such as restaurants, this normative behavior requires a subjugation of the self into the organizational power structure.

As presented in more detail elsewhere about power, looking at styles of decision-making, the general manager most often has the responsibility for making instant "top-down" decisions based on the their position power, while the area manager as a *leader of managers* must be more aware of the need for shared decision-making based on their need for follower power.

Position Power

For example, the Executive Chef has a job and a title which implies a higher position in the organization than would a cook or a dishwasher. The Chef has position or role power which comes with the job. Other employees implicitly accept this power relationship. This power is to be used by the Chef when they work in the organization, whether in making scheduling decisions, menu item choices, or taking actions that reward or punish individuals who are below them in the organization. We understand this when we see formal titles used, so a General has more power than a Captain and a Vice President is more powerful than a Restaurant Manager. This is position power and is seen every day in organizational life.

But in many ways there are two other bases for power in organizations that complement, and sometimes challenge the position power that comes with a title or role. The most easily seen is the power that comes from representing the organization itself, whether across the organizational boundaries to customers and suppliers or within the organizational system to internal stakeholders.

Organizational Power

For example, the clerk at the Department of Motor Vehicles, the ticket agent at the gate in the airport, or the voice on the other end of the Customer Service line, all have organizational power. This is also a form of bureaucratic power, where the authority of the individual is borrowed from the organization, the office, or even the function which they represent. Almost anytime an individual has the power to say "No" to another individual when enforcing a set of administrative rules, especially if there is little contextual control being exercised, this is organizational power.

Follower Power

The third power base is more difficult to define, but certainly just as, or more, important to the relationship between an individual and an organization. This power is shared by two people, the follower and the leader. It is shared in such a way as to appear being one sided, from the follower to the leader, but in fact it is an exchange with power being given by both sides. We can call this follower power, the power that individuals give to someone in and organization, whether they have an institutional power or not. This power does not come with a title, although the leader may also have an official or management title given by the organization and it does not come with the bureaucratic power of an office, although the leader may also speak for the organization as its official representative. The important thing is that neither is required for the access to this power base.

Contrasting Power Bases

The key to understanding how these three power bases are important to the *leader of managers* construct is to realize how they are applied in different ways by simple or complex situations. The founder/entrepreneur/owner of in an independent single unit may possess a combination of the three kinds of power and exercise control based upon them, but the balance will often be weighted in favor of individual charisma and personal style. There may be significant position power in an independent enterprise, the owner can certainly exercise their implied right to hire and fire or discipline an employee. But with a relatively small staff, the costs for such action can be high.

Likewise, there will be follower power given to the owner stemming from their personal role as the visionary or creative force in the enterprise. Entrepreneurs can effectively exert this power, typically more than the small business owner, because of the implied promise of growth and the strength they represent in presenting the previously mentioned "I've got an idea, let's go there...!" model of leadership. What they don't have is considerable organizational power, the organization they represent is often no larger than themselves.

Alternatively, as an organization grows in units and complexity, which is accompanied by the increase in employees, which leads to the growth of bureaucracy and administrative discipline, there is built-in organizational power. The multi-unit manager represents this organizational power, enhancing their role. When combined with an hierarchical structure which rewards people with titles and the implicit understanding that titles come with position power a change occurs. If the *leader of managers* gains follower power through the positive exchange of actions, vision and perceived value the effect becomes multiplied many times over.

4

Culture

Each organization has a dominant culture and usually a range of sub-cultures. Whether it is a small pizza shop or a multi-billion dollar conglomerate, all organizations communicate a set of shared beliefs that help them define values, moderate behaviors and set rules. For the *leader of managers* the understanding of a corporate culture becomes a crucial component of both control and advancement.

All organizations have their own particular cultures.

Each unique culture may be developed and grown by the organization's leadership, perhaps at the founding in a mission statement or organically as the company grows and finds its own character. But just as easily culture may be created by someone else in a management position within the enterprise who, because of charisma and follower power, steps up to define it for the entire organization. Not infrequently when these first two options are not chosen, then organizational cultures are co-opted by the employees themselves. When this third option occurs culture is entirely self-determined by natural leaders within the organization which may or may not match those of the original leadership. In each case values, norms and beliefs will be shared within the organization and a culture, strong or weak, good or bad, healthy or sick, will be formed.

Edger Schein, in presenting his seminal theories of how organizations controlled culture, defined corporate culture as:

> A pattern of basic assumptions—invented, discovered, or developed by a given group as it learns to cope with its problems of external adaptation and internal integration—that has

worked well enough to be considered valid and, therefore, to be taught to new members as the correct way to perceive, think, and feel in relation to those problems.

The reason this carries so much importance for the *leader of managers* is that culture fills in the organizational gaps otherwise left empty. By gap I mean the loose emotional spaces where people interact together with few written or spoken rules but with a mutually shared purpose. Culture can be viewed therefore as the glue which holds an organization together, the stronger the corporate culture the stronger the organization and the more

---

Teaching Culture:

1. What do leaders pay attention to, measure, and control?
2. How do leaders react to critical incidents & crises?
3. Are leaders deliberate role models, teachers, and coaches?
4. Is there balance of rewards and status?
5. Are stories told of recruitment, selection, promotion, retirement and banishment?

likely there will be clearly understood goals and forward progress. Where thought and purposeful decision-making have gone into the planning of a culture by senior leadership there will also be thought and purpose in the shared decisions made by all layers of the team when those leaders are not physically present to guide them.

Culture is a way of behaving, thinking, and acting that is learned and shared by an organization's members. Culture helps an organization to relate to the outside world, creating rules of normative behavior to aid employees in both boundary setting and boundary spanning. At the same time culture moderates internal behaviors and helps build ways for people within the organization to relate to each other.

Culture is important in four key ways:

1) Culture strategically encourages employee commitment by offering them a sense of higher purpose, of being a part of an organization which is bigger than they are, and which holds a set of core values they can choose to share and build upon. Culture can be inspirational.

2) Culture, when managed effectively, can become a competitive advantage. Because no manager can ever be 100% involved in every single aspect of an organization's activities culture becomes a management decision tool when it acts as a

moderator of individual employee behaviors. Culture can act like an organization's conscience.

3) A strong culture can help to give employees a useful system of guideposts and borderlines for dealing with each other in their own working subunits, with the broader organization itself, and with individuals external to the company including customers, suppliers or the media. Culture both sets limits and expands horizons.

4) Culture can become a core competency for any company, especially where a positive culture is recognized by outsiders as a desirable part of the organization. Companies named as "best employer" or are given other accolades from external sources often find it easier to recruit, retain and promote employees who seek to become part of the organization and ultimately self-identify with the culture itself. Culture defines a brand.

Organizational subcultures

Left to their own within a dominant organizational culture, groups both large and small will also form subcultures. Many companies know that they have both a formal culture which will appear as the public face shown to the outside world, and an informal culture which reflects the many private realities within a company. The Finance Department will have a special way of conducting its daily work just as the Marketing or Operations departments will have theirs.

As an illustration, think of any family. The neighbors will have an impression of what the family is like (the public face) but inside the family itself (the private reality) there may be one culture for the entire group, but then one shared by the adults, one created by the children, possibly one built around the male family members and another for the females. It isn't that there are secrets, although there may be, so much as there are different symbols, stories, sometimes even different languages that are used to include or exclude those family members who are not in that particular culture at that moment.

In an organization, as these cultures are being formed shared teachings become shared beliefs, values and norms about how interactions in the organization should be conducted. Beliefs form the ideological core values of any culture. Values are preferences for certain behaviors or certain outcomes over others. Norms are standards of behavior that define how people are expected to act while part of the organization. When they are important enough norms may be codified and written down. The emerging culture will both reflect and determine which values are important to current members and which should be carried forward to future members. It will describe what activities and

actions have worth and are encouraged to be repeated and which
are not valued at all. Over time, these shared beliefs become the
norms which drive all members' behaviors.

Two personal examples of a "subculture" at work

Positive Sub-Culture: When we owned our restaurant in
Maitland, Florida, the partners tried to make it very clear that we
did not consider the restaurant to be a "private dining room" for
our personal use. We established from the beginning that all of us
would pay full price for anything we ordered—meals, drinks,
pizza to go—every time we entered the premises. It was well
known that even sharing a simple glass of iced tea with a friend
would require a guest check. There were no discounts and no
"freebies" when we visited; we were running a business first and
foremost. This behavior meant that not only the owners but
management and all employees were respectful of this cultural
value. They tended not to give away or take advantage of our
policies, even though another policy we emphasized "make sure
every guest leaves happy" would normally be at odds with the no
"free" expectation. Employees knew we believed that all guest
complaints required immediate attention, but not all guest
complaints required something to be "on the house" to make
them satisfied though if it did everyone was empowered to make
the offer. Over time, most of our staff became more mindful of

the use and abuse of our no free food and beverage policy than the partners did simply because the staff was enforcing a cultural norm which they believed they themselves had established.

Negative Sub-Culture: Alternatively, many years before that I was working as a waiter at a new and very popular restaurant in Boston. Like all of the experienced senior wait staff, I had recently managed a fine-dining restaurant before taking the job and was serving simply because the money was so much better than anything else I could do at the time. The "house" had strict policies written in manuals dealing with behaviors from cash control to service style. But there was also extreme pressure placed on the dining room managers by the hands-on, but very inexperienced, ownership for both increasing revenues and total loyalty. This pressure meant that there was a "revolving door" where new managers were often replaced within weeks of starting the position.

What most of these people did not understand at the time was that a subculture had evolved because the owners trusted the waiters more than the new managers and relied on us to let them know who should stay and who should go. In fact, the experienced front of house staff met informally to set its own rules for daily work activities, including everything from our shift scheduling to the system for wine controls. While it was empowering for the staff to be part of the "family" and have such direct access to the owners, this was a very unhealthy environment for both the management team and the long-term financial success of the business.

Laws, Language, Stories and Heroes

So, in order for the *leader of managers* to control the dominant culture, as well as the various subcultures in the organization, communication of shared beliefs needs to be planned and implemented. This communication comes in many forms. An experienced *leader of managers* knows that at various times they may use a combination of styles; communicating through laws, language, symbols, stories and myths, legends and heroes, and ultimately rituals, each of which must be designed and controlled by the effective organization.

Laws are the rules, policies or regulations that all organizations have created and put into a formal structure. Basically these are the norms which are so important they need to be written down, to make codified what might simply be verbally shared but need to become part of an organization's collective long-term memory. All operating manuals, human resource policies, maintenance procedures, websites, employee newsletters and any standardized forms or custom software applications would all be considered examples of laws for enhancing culture.

To share these laws each organization develops an internal language or lingo of its own, which is frequently incomprehensible to outsiders. The internal lexicon may include technical terms, simple abbreviations or acronyms, and the shorthand slang which enables rapid internal comprehension. This language may be adopted from external sources, such as in medical or legal circles, or it may be developed internally at the smallest unit level of just a handful of employees such as a group of kitchen prep cooks or inspectors in a remote field office.

Symbols are also part of this shared language and become the physical objects or artifacts that have significance beyond their obvious meaning. These symbols can be in the form of icons, totems, signs or other manifestations. Sports team locker rooms are places where symbolic meaning is easily spotted, where old uniforms, statutes, or pieces of used equipment may take on special meaning long after they appear. Brand management relies heavily on the use of symbolic meaning for communicating with external customers, but symbols may also be used effectively in the same way with internal customers to define organizational culture.

In stronger cultures a part of this language will evolve into myth making through the creation of stories and the identification of organizational legends and heroes. These stories are usually transmitted to foster positive behaviors and actions among the members of the organization. Sharing stories and identifying heroes are two important reasons an organization holds an annual convention. A gathering of like-minded individuals in one place is a highly efficient means for disseminating stories across the entire population.

One avenue to take in surfacing cultural touchstones is to identify company heroes. Finding those heroes and legends, like so many of the other principles we have covered in this book, is also very lifecycle dependent. At early entrepreneurial stages of organizational growth, the visionary founder will often be the "hero" who everyone tells stories about. Later as more units are opened, the newest hero might emerge as the one general manager who went the extra mile during a hurricane and kept her unit open during the storm. As the company expands still later heroic actions happen in the burgeoning corporate office as the CFO lands venture capital financing. Eventually, the founder starts to become more of a mythical figure than a simply heroic one, and the legends are woven to support more ideal behaviors from the staff.

Every organization also creates and practices rituals, those symbolic acts that people perform to gain and maintain membership or identity within a culture. Meetings are a ritual.

How they are conducted, where they are conducted, and who sets the meeting agenda are very informative ways of conveying an organizational culture. Company ceremonies, whether to bestow awards for meeting sales goals, banquets celebrating years of employee service at retirement, or the cutting of a ribbon in front of a new unit as it opens, are all rituals which reinforce organizational beliefs and shared values. As a society we have weddings to celebrate the belief in the institution of marriage, we hold graduations to celebrate the value of education, and funerals to honor and remember. Leaders of any organization chose which beliefs are so important as an integral component of their culture that members need to celebrate them as rituals.

What I would suggest is that if you as the *leader of managers* want to understand your culture, you need to identify the heroes that other employees admire. You will want to listen to the stories being told that are starting to become legends, and from those legends listen for the stories turning into the myths that reinforce core values. You will then be able to discern what employees think are the underlying cultural beliefs, shared values and normative behaviors they feel should be emulated in their daily routines. Then the understanding of dominant and sub-cultural language, symbols and rituals will be beneficial for the development of a strong organization as it grows.

We all learn critical behaviors by watching the actions of those around us, especially by observing those who have come before and have an historical perspective on what brings success. When the *leader of managers* is successful in surfacing these cultural norms there is the possibility to use them as a "soft" control mechanism, a tool to support and nurture the health of the growing organization.

5

Life Cycle of the Organization and the Executive

"To everything there is a season..."

In the study of management we have come to recognize that organizations in the business environment mimic living organisms in nature—there is birth, a period of growth, a time of maturity, and eventually decline. There is solid evidence to suggest that the theory of business lifecycles can be very relevant for strategy setting and planning.

Similarly, the study of marketing recognizes that products, and now services, also have a lifecycle. New products are introduced to the market, have a period of trial use, growth and market acceptance, often leading to a time of flattening sales and commoditization. Marketers use the theory of product lifecycles to set sales objectives, begin new product rollouts or redesign, and for setting promotion and advertising budgets.

We take this idea one step further and suggest that the theory of lifecycles should also apply to the skills of the manager who leads the organization through its various stages of development. As a business moves from birth to old age in a series of increasingly more complex steps, we propose that individual managers are best suited, due to their own style and characteristics, to fit along an organization's lifecycle curve. Simply put, great companies match *the right person to the right place in the right time* for each strategic business unit they control.

Finding the right place for your team of managers, or even for yourself, becomes not just a matter of theoretical interest, it becomes a crucial aspect of the management of diverse organizations and diverse talent. Restaurant companies are complex service organizations which require complex management strategies. No single individual can be expected to be "right" for every level of the organization over time.

For a number of years Tom Peters has said that we should all manage our businesses as if we were the owners of a major league sports team. To win in Premier Football, a team needs to have the very best players and the very top coaches. Some teams are in the "building" stage creating future players, others use "seasoned" veterans to provide maturity and experience during highly competitive late season games. The same is true of building a world-class restaurant company. New young talent needs to be used to help build growing teams while seasoned veterans add market knowledge and perspective.

If we look at the stages represented in **Figure 15** the Leadership Life Cycle graphic, you will see that both the organization and the style of leadership needed for the six stages change and evolve as the concept moves through time. Each stage of the development has a different set of opportunities and threats for the parent organization.

Industry Recognition of Lifecycle Leaders

A good way to visualize these various stages is to think about an industry conference and the kinds of activities and presentations that might be listed on the event program. That a panel of "Hot Concepts of Tomorrow" would most likely be represented by firms in Stages 1 or 2 of the Life Cycle. Those companies named as last year's "Growth Leaders" in terms of number of new units and/or percentage of increasing revenues would probably be in either Stage 3 or 4 on the curve.

When you listen to a group of company presidents on a "Leadership Panel" they are most likely representatives of organizations in Stage 5. When a person is honored with a "Lifetime Achievement Award" at the evening banquet it is almost always some past leader who is firmly in Stage 6.

As in the building of any structure, a great foundation supports the construction that rises from it. We can easily see that as an organization grows, leaders at each stage become the "Support Columns" for the enterprise. We build great companies on the strength of the people who lead our teams. Let us, then, take a look at the specific characteristics which are important for each Stage.

Stage 1—The Creator/Entrepreneur

Stage 1 is the time of the Creator/Entrepreneur, the person seeking new ideas, the seer of what has been called by Drucker the "Seam of Opportunity" in a market place. These are the

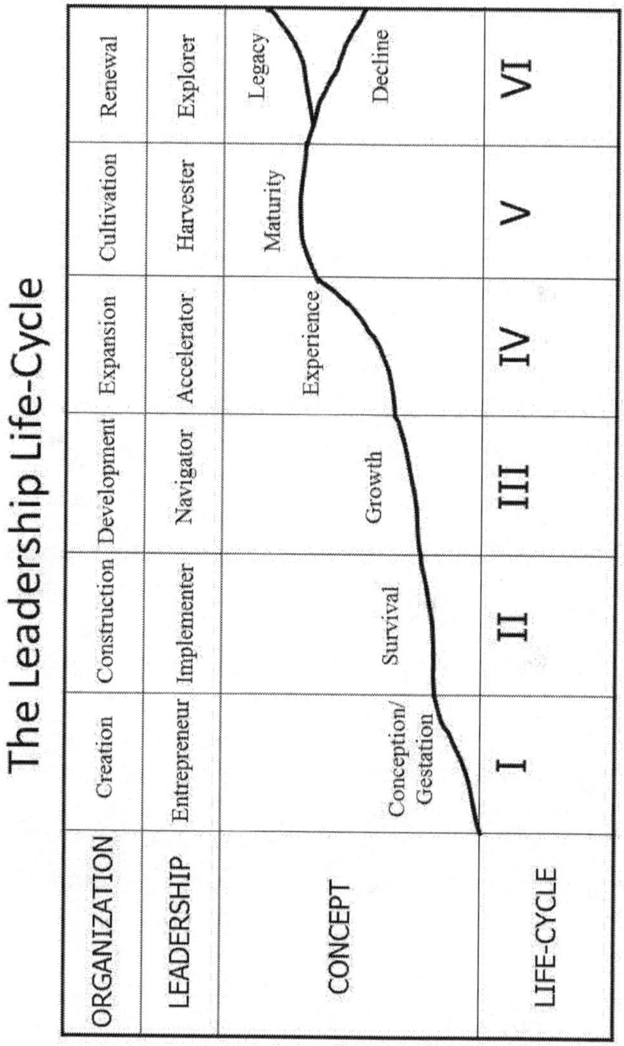
The Leadership Life-Cycle
ORGANIZATION
Creation
Construction
Development
Expansion
Cultivation
Renewal
LEADERSHIP
Entrepreneur
Implementer
Navigator
Accelerator
Harvester
Explorer
CONCEPT
Conception/ Gestation
Survival
Growth
Experience
Maturity
Legacy
Decline
LIFE-CYCLE
I
II
III
IV
V
VI

Figure 15

people who lead the organization from conception through gestation and guide the birth process. They are pioneers, experimental, charismatic, often looking for the "buzz" that comes from innovation and adaptation.

Often these individuals are looked at by society as high-risk takers, but in surveys they see themselves as risk avoiders—for them it is simply too risky not to make the creative leap with a new concept because the market will pass them by if they wait. When you hear someone say, "I've got a great idea! Come with me!" you are observing a Stage 1 leader.

The positive attributes for this kind of leader include passion, focus, confidence, stability, tenacity and high levels of energy. All make them highly motivational. Where they have negative attributes, often it involves a tendency to become distracted, discouraged or to spread themselves thin and have their energy diluted. The focus of the organization at this stage is typically external, channeled into capturing new customers at the unit level. The prime market for this stage is a local first time trial user.

Stage 2—The Rationalizer/Implementer

Stage 2 is the time of the construction managers, the people who bring a "rational" form to the organization. This is the specialty of the Implementer, the refiner of the new concept, the creator of the essence of the brand and the one who sees the core of the new idea and gives it character. These are the creators of an organizational culture on which will be built a new organization. This is also a time that will test the very survival of the new organization as it reaches beyond its home base, its comfort zone, and starts the construction of new units in new areas.

There is still tremendous energy in the level of commitment from these leaders, but they also exhibit a different set of positive attributes than in Stage 1. They bring communication skills, determination, quality mindedness, strong problem solving abilities and a vision for organizational development. Both the organization and the leader at this stage may exhibit the negative attributes of being under-capitalized (monetarily and emotionally). They may be driving growth for growth alone, which often leads to shoddiness of decision-making and an acceptance of lower standards. The focus of this stage turns internal, seeking to find a way to replicate the existing original business. Markets for Stage 2 are finding loyal customers who are already returning and making them more frequent users.

Stage 3—The Systemizer/Navigator

It is in Stage 3 where the real work of organizational development begins. This is the time of the Systemizer/Navigator, the person who brings order out of chaos. Like an engineer they create standards and processes, refine distribution channels, direct the creation of operating manuals and control systems, build teams and support programs, and initiate franchise networks and put forward growth plans. These leaders have positive attributes that show themselves in the development of planning, administration, relationship building, staff education, and developing big picture visions.

At this time the risk of negative behaviors tend to be personal paralysis, over-confidence, and self-satisfaction. The focus of the leader and the business remain internal, requiring a passion for systematically getting every product right, with uniformity, consistency, and competence shown across the entire system. The markets for the Stage 3 firm are now regional and reach across multiple units and across multiple areas.

Stage 4—The Accelerator/Builder

Things really begin to explode in Stage 4. It is the realm of the Accelerator/Builder, the grower of large companies. These are the true corporate entrepreneurs, building and opening new units and new markets. They live the biblical admonition to 'be fruitful and multiply.' During the time of the Accelerator companies undergo rapid growth, creating opportunities and economies of both scale and scope. These are the leaders who are masters of delegation, knowing that in order to grow control has to be shared. They are forceful, pragmatic and highly achievement motivated.

It is their experience in managing complex organizations that helps the enterprise to grow in new but controlled ways. Risks associated with this style of leadership include the possibilities of over-reaching, inflexibility, a desire to keep to the plan, and defections of staff members who might have been passed by in the rapid growth of the organization.

The focus of the Accelerator shifts from internal issues to external ones, as they are consumed by finding avenues to fuel growth. New markets, new sites, new opportunities are the drivers of the mission. This external vision is characterized by the organization's rush to 'find all the customers' not just those from the original target group. The market now is national, seeking to have an increasing number of customers come in more frequently.

Stage 5—Steward/Harvester

Eventually, as in any lifecycle model, growth will slow down and reach a plateau, a peak that starts to flatten. This is when the Accelerator is replaced by the Steward/Harvester. After a period of rapid growth there needs to be a time of reaping the outcome, of taking stock of what has occurred and creating true wealth. Stewardship is about managing a business that is healthy, still vibrant, and being strengthened for a long and prosperous future. Shareholder value is important, as is brand extension, and financial stability. Harvesters "manage the margins" cultivating a business of sustained profitability through professional planning, forecasting and asset appreciation. Here the key attributes of the leader are competitiveness, consistency, character and personal charisma.

Unfortunately, mature companies can, through too much harvesting and not enough growing, become flat. The negative attributes of the leader in this Stage 5 are such things as egotism, comfort with the status quo, entropy, and slow erosion of business. Similarly, the focus has turned back to internal affairs, seeking to maintain market share through existing core competencies with little or no erosion. The market is now universal, focused on a wide core customer base, basically 'anyone' who can use our products.

The final stage is both similar to, and can be very different than, a living organism. In biology, all things pass from maturity into old age and eventual death. In the marketplace organizations have the good fortune to be able to continually renew themselves and extend their lives beyond a single generation.

Stage 6—Caregivers or Rejuvenator/Explorer

This offers us two separate Stage 6 leadership styles. Those who take a slowly declining business into its final stages are the Hospice Caregivers, making sure that the organization's life support systems are fully functioning, that pain is minimal, and that when the end is near, vital pieces (like organs donated for transplantation) are harvested for their value. These people are deconstructionists, focusing on internal issues, and relying on loyal customers to support the business to the end, which will eventually happen.

The alternative, and more desirable leader for the long-term health of the organization, is the Rejuvenator/Explorer. This person is focused on re-energizing the organization from top to bottom, often called a Turnaround Specialist by the media. Not unlike a surgeon they may remove life-threatening tissue to aid in the survival of the patient. They are the builders on a legacy, using the knowledge of the past to find a new future. They will explore new opportunities, and seek new ways to find new paths to follow. These leaders are inquisitive, self-assured, opportunistic and seekers of innovation. They turn the focus of the organization to the outside, looking for new trial users and new areas to master.

So, what are we to learn from this lifecycle model? The primary message is that it is probably the rare leader who can guide a company from birth to renewal. Each stage of your organization's lifecycle brings with it a complexity and set of challenges that will respond to a particular leadership style. As well, as managers in your organization move with it through the lifecycle stages, they really are confronted by two choices; they have shown skills that are applicable, or they must learn and adopt new sets of competencies and attributes.

I suggest that while it is possible to learn one or two stages worth of these competencies, few individuals have the ability to master all six. Senior management must not only be aware of their own strengths as they lead an organization, but they must be able to identify the strengths of the people who are helping to lead with them. Having the wrong person in the wrong place will inevitably mean that they will fail in the position. In both situations, underestimation of skills or misplacement of talent, the organization stands to lose a valuable asset. Like any other asset, the human capital which is invested in the wrong place produces a lower than desired return, and in the worst scenario, it produces a loss.

What we should all desire instead is for our organizations to have the strategic vision to recycle and renew our best leaders, treating them like the assets they are. The best organizations create both options for their talent, offering ways to gain new competencies for those who are able to learn them, and fresh opportunities to build on clearly identified existing leadership skills.

6

The "Black Hole"

There is a special time in the growth of multi-unit enterprises, which unfortunately often catches founders and entrepreneurs by surprise. I have been using the term the "Black Hole" of restaurant growth, but I have also been fond of the name the "Bermuda Triangle" in the life cycle (both have a similar point—companies go in but don't come out). In the early entrepreneurial stage of development it is taken for granted that new enterprises have zero revenues and large opening expenses, this is the risky part of opening any business (see **Figures 16 & 17** below).

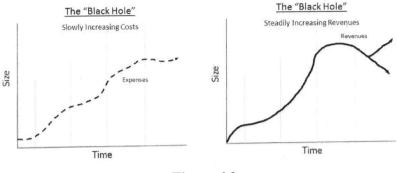

Figure 16

But, if things go well and the marketplace demands growth, revenues begin to increase much faster than expenses which will still continue to increase. During this point, which for many businesses is the time from 2 to 10 units, excitement can run very high, as can the pressure to expand quite rapidly.

That is where a confluence of challenging issues come together and may create a metaphorical flood. One of the first things to happen is that expenses begin to grow quickly as the need for investment in infrastructure becomes crucial.

Specifically, as described earlier in this section, with growth comes the need for new employees to be brought on board, many to support the growing headquarters staff. With each increase in the span of control, around 5-8 new units, a new *leader of managers* must be hired, trained and supported. As territories expand, so does the need to support travel for site visits, training

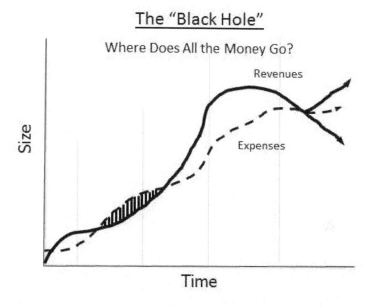

Figure 17

for new managers and owners, as well as new crew members. Operating manuals need to be created as systems are introduced. Marketing expenses increase, information technologies are demanded, and meetings must be held at off-site locations. Sooner, rather than later, a larger space must be acquired for the corporate headquarters (or Operations Support Center, Home Office, or whatever special name it is given).

All of this is occurring while the "best and the brightest" from older units, each of which has its own product lifecycle of maturity to contend with, are helping to drive the bright new unit openings. Revenues at existing units become flat from a natural lack of attention, while new units cannot be opened fast enough to increase revenues above opening expenses, and investment in non-revenue producing infrastructure is happening at breakneck speed.

It is into the Black Hole that many "hot concept" companies rush, never to be seen or heard from again. If, and this is the ultimate big "if" question, there has been planning well in advance for this time period, with significant capital resources secured in advance, multi-unit companies may come out on the other end as revenues quickly catch up and then grow faster than expenses. Referring to the Leadership Lifecycle in **Figure 15** one of the most tragic outcomes of this challenge is that the well-meaning founder of the enterprise will have been completely blind-sided by this experience and will be a casualty of the process.

Surviving the Bermuda Triangle of growth should be every entrepreneurial company's ultimate goal, and the true lesson to be learned from the Lifecycle concept.

Part Four

BECOMING THE LEADER OF MANAGERS

(and the Manager of Leaders)

Study the hard while it is easy.
Do big things while they are small.
The hardest jobs in the world start out easy,
the great affairs of the world start small.
So the wise soul,
by never dealing with great things,
gets great things done.
-Lao Tzu, Tao Te Ching

"Promote revolutionary ideas under cover of
evolutionary change."
Rosabeth Moss Kanter

The Four Keys

After all we have revealed about the Market, the Individual and the Organization, we need to present an action plan to illustrate the way in which the new *Leader of Managers* can bring everything into practice. These are the four key areas to consider:

1) Become a *Catalyst for Change* and identify the challenges which are confronting your organization. No great leader ever became great by maintaining the status quo.

2) In order for you to lead other managers in a process of change you must provide a *Clarity of Vision*, a clear path toward the future for your team and the people they in turn will lead.

3) Your vision must be *Focused on People* especially those who are inside the "magic square meter" where the service worker and the customer meet. You must take the time to manage. By this I mean knowing when you should act tactically and when you should be strategic. You must know when you are needed as a leader, but also when you are needed as a manager or when you are needed as an administrator. These different roles are not superior or inferior to one another. Great leaders intuitively comprehend the time to apply the right role to each situation as it is necessary.

4) You will need to understand the role of the *Servant Leader* who in the words of Robert Greenleaf "serves so others may lead and leads so others may serve." I suggest reflecting on a simple question will help you in this task. Every morning as you look in the mirror ask yourself the same thing, "What can I do today that will make their jobs easier and more meaningful?"

There are four essential ideas to address in detail: change; vision; people; and service.

1

An Agent for Change

Change is inevitable, in the physical world of things as well as the organizational world of people. One role of the leader in an organization is to be a catalyst for that change. As in the physical world, there are two basic forms that change may take when applied to organizations. One is *endothermic*, requiring energy from the outside, and one is *exothermic*, releasing energy from the inside.

A very simplistic way to explain this would be to highlight the difference between a traditional oven, where the heat bakes from the outside to the inside, and a microwave oven, where the heat radiates from the inside to the outside. A cake baked in an oven slowly gets firm and browns on the outside yet stays moist on the inside, while one baked in a microwave will be firm on the inside but will never form a browned crust. On the other hand, reheating lasagna in the microwave will instantly bring the center up to a safe temperature without burning the cheese on the top; something a traditional oven would never be capable of doing.

Each has its purpose, but the outcomes are very different. The same can be said for leaders and the way they manage change.

The leader as **Change Agent** is all about taking the people she/he leads to a new future. In **Figure 18** the means to effect that change is the Catalyst—the *leader of managers*—who through her actions and the application of Behaviors (new practices), Skills (new abilities), or Knowledge (new ideas) multiplies the effects of the decisions she makes. The catalyst as a Change Agent is seeking to create or implement new business models and products, new management models of structures and activities, or new process models of leadership and systems so that these new outcomes become part of the organization.

In some situations this change will be forced on individuals within the organization, coerced by a *leader of managers* when he/she applies energy (heat or pressure) from outside the business unit core. In other situations change will be generated from within the organization through small teams of highly motivated people or even individual activists who have responded to a vision and call for change. Clearly, either option can be effective. But just as in the use of different ovens for different application of heat, different styles of management and leadership will yield a variety of professional outcomes.

The **Catalyst** for change can begin either an Endothermic (*outside—in*) reaction or an Exothermic (*inside—out*) reaction. In both cases the Change Agent must be aware of, and prepared for, the opportunity for change to implement new outcomes.

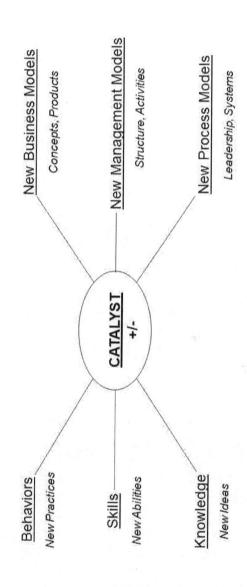

CATALYST
+/-

New Business Models
Concepts, Products

New Management Models
Structure, Activities

New Process Models
Leadership, Systems

Behaviors
New Practices

Skills
New Abilities

Knowledge
New Ideas

Figure 18

The Four Faces of Change

This brings us to an interesting point. What do we know of change? I would suggest to you that there are four faces of change: Anticipated, Unexpected, Transitional and Catastrophic. Each has its own time horizon. Each comes with risk and reward, although in much different ratios. We ask our leaders to manage the uncertainties of the future, to set forth a vision and a clear path for us that considers each of these four faces of change.

The Anticipated Change is the one upon which we build our business models. We act as if at least one truth is a solid foundation stone on which we may construct a structure. We do this in order to show that as a manager we have some control over the future and can anticipate and make predictions about what we know will come. This anticipated change allows us to forecast, to budget, and to write multi-year strategic plans. "I know what has been, I am aware of things today, I can therefore prognosticate about what will be, and then can construct my world with a measure of certainty." We do, in fact, require insight and foresight, and reward senior executives when

Four Faces of Change

Anticipated:	Unexpected:
Forecasted	*Alternatives*
Transitional:	Catastrophic:
Evolutionary	*Life Altering*

they master them. "Vision" is revealed when we predict the future and minimize organizational risk by relying on our knowledge and abilities to anticipate change.

The restaurant business is notable because it regularly exhibits a highly predictable seasonality, but actual guest counts each evening are very random. For example, for most restaurants Friday night will be busier than Tuesday, and dinner will be busiest from 6:00 until 8:00 each evening. The exact number of patrons in any given meal period will be arbitrary, one Friday night might have 200 guests and the next Friday it could be 215, but it will be relatively the same each week. The anticipated number of guests gives management the confidence to accurately schedule staff, order cases of wine and prepare food for the expected nightly demand.

The Transitional Change is the trend that happens with little obvious notice but occurs over a longer period of time. This, like the Anticipated Change, would be considered a future with some knowable expected outcomes because it often is based on demographic shifts, emerging technologies, or cyclical economic activity. In the world we live in, I would call this "rapid but hardly noticed" change. The acceptance of smartphones in the U.S. is an example. In 2013 more than 57% of all cell phones in use are smartphones, up from just 35% in 2011. We can all reasonably predict that smartphone and tablet use will continue to expand over the coming decade.

Consumer behaviors over the past fifty years have changed gradually, then dramatically and in some cases very rapidly. But because they are so universal, most of these changes seem organic and evolutionary, not abrupt. For example, the U.S. Surgeon General released his warning about smoking and health in January, 1964. Today open smoking in restaurants seems a relic of a time gone by, but public no-smoking policies are still not universal and have only been in effect in places such as NYC and Florida since 2003. Consumer product life cycles, at one time almost a generation in length, may now need refurbishment and renewal in just three to five years.

The same, of course, is true in the restaurant environment. Consumer choices can shift quite rapidly, fortunately so can the ability of the industry to match those changes. Total coffee consumption in the U.S. was near historic lows by the late 1980's. Then over the past thirty years the emergence of Starbuck's has awakened the marketplace (literally) and coffee in all variations is again one of the favored drinks. Rivals such as Dunkin' Donuts and McDonald's have benefited greatly from reacting forcefully to this transitional trend.

Evolutionary change such as this doesn't happen overnight or appear as a fad, it has been a steady process. Rosabeth Moss Kanter says, "Promote revolutionary ideas under cover of evolutionary change." Leading during a time of transitional change can help to turn a long-term vision into a reality. The leadership behaviors that slowly unfold over a year or longer, which take into account that attitudes and behaviors also change, are best matched to the transitional change.

These changes, which are basically long-term trend lines, can be both a blessing and a curse. The leader who fails to see and react to the evolutionary change will suddenly be confronted with choices that are no longer relevant.

The Unexpected Change is the one we know is coming, but we simply don't know what it will look like, and is therefore the item that most causes tension and fear of the unknown. This is the face we look into when we create Alternative Futures, when we do a "Worst Case Scenario" or ask, "What if...?" An accomplished chess player is at a different level of play than a chess master. The player looks at the board and anticipates the next few moves. The master looks at the board and even knowing which moves are most likely to come, still takes nothing for granted and plans multiple possible outcomes. So it is with the *leader of managers* who considers the Unexpected Change and creates alternative futures in case one should occur.

The leader who sets in place a clear and detailed set of plans for the future, but includes a review process in case those plans do not work, will be seen as better prepared than one with only one path to success. Employee trust is built on a pattern of sound decisions, especially when times of adversity arise.

Examples of managing unexpected change include the purchase of business interruption insurance to cover employee salaries in case of a major event such as hurricane or staff training sessions for simple events such as a power failure. Prepared leaders know that the unexpected will eventually happen and they have envisioned alternative futures, termed emergency planning, before they occur. Sometimes, though, even the best of planning cannot predict completely random events.

No one wants to be faced with a <u>Catastrophic Change</u>, the one that is life altering or even life destroying. These events, most often beyond the ability of anyone to predict outside of science fiction, still do occur, and can often include a tragic loss. The death of a founder, the complete loss from fire, or other seemingly arbitrary act of nature or man, can have a devastating impact on the business.

The key to dealing with these "storm of the century" events, the event that no amount of planning can ever foresee, is to be prepared for all inevitable possibilities. The goal for the leader is to turn what for others would be a catastrophic change into an unexpected change—one where multiple alternative choices are already in place. This is the moment that calls for crisis management.

Response time during a catastrophic event is accelerated, solid information is always limited or even unavailable, but the *leader of managers* must be available to explain, control, and influence the emotions and calm the fears of those they lead. This is the face of change no one wants to see, but if not anticipated will often be the make or break point of a career.

Most recently we could see that the real difference between the response to a catastrophic crisis in New Orleans, with no real advanced preparation for Hurricane Katrina, and in the New York City/New Jersey metro region with detailed advanced planning for Hurricane Sandy, was the human cost. Instead of over a thousand people being killed, most of the terrible damage was suffered by buildings. The unthinkable devastation and flooded subways had been in fact thought about and prepared for, no matter how bad the reality became. Clearly the effects on property and lives were tragic in New York and along the Jersey Shore, but lives were not lost because of a lack of foresight.

2

Clarity of Vision

Leadership was born when the first human pointed and said, "I think we should go over there…" and everyone did.

But pointing in a direction and having people follow you isn't simply about moving west across the wilderness from the harbor in Boston to the harbor in San Francisco. Physical movement is certainly a part of leadership. So is the emotional task of taking an organization in a new strategic direction. Having a vision, and convincing people to share it are two very different things. In both cases, physical and emotional, movement and action will only happen when the followers have faith in the clarity of the leader's vision for the future. It requires trust that the new path forward is well designed. It requires a belief that the leader is acting with the best intentions for bringing success to the team. As Marcus Buckingham notes, "Great leaders rally people to a better future."

```
┌─────────────────────────────────────────────┐
│              Two Perspectives                │
│                                              │
│   MANAGER                      LEADER        │
│                                              │
│   • Stability      ◄──────►    • Change      │
│                                              │
│   • Order          ◄──────►    • Clarity     │
│                                              │
│   • Focused on     ◄──────►    • Focused on  │
│     the Individual               Collective  │
│     Employee                     Action      │
│                                              │
└─────────────────────────────────────────────┘
```

In Part Two we discussed the important part the perceptions of thee three power bases play in the internal relationship each LOM has when fulfilling the leader, manager and the administrator roles. I suggested there was a fluidity among the roles as each needed to be taken on for specific reasons and at specific times. So how does the *leader of managers* build the trust that is necessary so that people will believe in the vision and follow her?

The balance we have discussed previously is at this fulcrum point where clarity of vision is concerned. As a manager, the LOM needs to be focused in the moment and on the individual. As long ago as 1979 Kenneth Kovach found that the three top motivators for workers were: 1) Appreciation for the work being done; 2) Sympathetic help with personal problems; and 3) Having a feeling of being in on things in the workplace.

Other similar studies, recently Amabile and Kramer on the "Inner Work Life" or Grant on the role of focused "prosocial" goals have shown that leaders have a strong impact on employee motivation and productivity mostly through non-financial decisions.

Ultimately, trust is established when employees feel secure in their work, when they feel trusted themselves, and when they trust in the expertise of their manager. To accomplish these things, managers want to establish workplace stability, bring a sense of order from organizational chaos, and to focus on employee needs one at a time.

The challenge is that the leader needs to control necessary change while maintaining stability, use systems and order in a way to help define a clear vision, and to create a sense of team purpose and collective action one employee at a time. Quite a challenge.

How can this challenge be met? The *leader of managers* is given three tools, Charisma, Expertise and Composure to use on a daily basis.

Charisma is the tool that allows leaders to engage in the art of persuasion to accomplish their goals. There may be times where direct orders will be necessary, where the power of the position is enough, but where the span of control is wide, direct orders can be forgotten or never heard as soon as the LOM leaves the building. Persuasion, on the other hand allows for enlightened self-interest by the employee. This can often be enhanced in the service environment with an underlying message of what is termed "prosocial" behavior, pursuing a vision that is other directed and beneficial for a greater good.

> **Charisma:**
> capacity to inspire followers with devotion and enthusiasm.
>
> *Concise Oxford Dictionary*

Expertise is based on followers believing in the native intelligence of the leader. "This person will make good decisions because they are smart and have great experience." Where this is especially important is in response to uncertainty and anxiety about the future felt by those being led. A history of good, intelligent decision-making increases the likelihood of acceptance of the vision, and the willingness to embark on the journey from here to there.

Composure is the way a leader comports themselves, the behavior modeling when they are in front of employees. Self-confidence but not ego, containment but not aloofness, being centered and calm when under stress or in crisis are the characteristics of the visionary leader.

A clear, concise, and controlled message by a persuasive, intelligent and self-confident leader will always help to define the vision for the future, no matter how unknown the path.

3

Focused Champion

Earlier using the **5 Phases Model** we presented the concept that the highest order of concept mastery is Human Resource Management. By this we mean that one must accept the full-time commitment of the *leader of managers* to being the **Focused Champion** of your people, a developer of human capital and fully people oriented for results.

Consider this: think of the world of professional sports management. Suppose you had just purchased the *Number Two* football team in the world with the intention of becoming

Number One. As the new owner what would be the very first thing you would review to increase the value of your investment? Would you look at the team roster or the concessions contract? Which would you choose as a priority—to meet with the head coach or the head of buildings and grounds?

Great sports teams are first and foremost collections of highly skilled people with very specific talents who are allowed to perform at their very best. I suggest as the new team owner you would immediately focus on the "inventory of people" which comprises your team, from the head coach to the benchwarmer, to figure out who were the highest contributors to the team's success.

The very next thing you would consider is the bench strength of your team, the depth of future talent that you will need to replace a current player, or to look to when you build your roster next season. Who will be the next superstar, the new team leader on the field, or the role player that is the heart of another championship season?

Isn't that also how you should see your team as the *leader of managers*? As the coach, not the player, your job is to focus on finding the best people you can to fill the management positions in your organization. Your job is to encourage the people who report to you to stand up, take charge, and do the things they wouldn't do without your encouragement. You need to give them the courage to act, and the freedom to perform at their very best.

This encouragement is revealed to them through the behaviors and practices you model, through the verbal and non-verbal messages you send, and by the questions and topics you set as priorities. It is a well-known maxim that the person who sets the agenda at a meeting is the person with the power. You need to set the agenda for your organization, and it needs to have talent development as the number one priority.

Nine Key *Leader of Managers* Tactics

1. Communicate the Big Picture
2. Delegate Work and Responsibility
3. Help Employees Set Goals
4. Recognize Causes Not Symptoms
5. Reward Employees For Doing the Right Things
6. Be a Mentor
7. Give Meaningful, Timely, and Accurate Feedback
8. Have a Heart
9. Take Time to Be a Manager

Marcus Buckingham in *The One Thing You Need to Know (2005)* writes that the goal of a manager is "to excel at turning one person's talent into performance." He then suggests that "great leaders rally people to a better future." I would suggest that bonding the two together, supporting positive performance with a focus on the future is at the core of the *leader of managers* success. This is the highway to achieving great things together.

A significant beginning in this journey is to understand that delegation is a training tool for individual development, not simply a means to pass along tasks to underlings. Delegating both the responsibility for completing a project and the authority necessary to ensure the project reaches a successful conclusion is a management practice that enhances both your competence as a leader and the competence of those who work with you as future leaders. It will always be cheaper and more efficient to simply tell someone what to do. But it will never have as positive a long-term impact as involving him in the decision process and the ownership of the outcome of that decision.

The *leader of managers* who engages in this behavior will come to realize that people think that they work "with" rather than "for" them because most of their time is taken up by people rather than tasks and products.

As that focus on people is reinforced, guest satisfaction becomes the primary motivator for the entire team. As noted previously, the single most important piece of real estate in the portfolio is the **magic square meter** where the face of the company, the service employee, and the guest interact. As Albrecht & Zemke noted in 1985, "If you aren't serving a customer, you better be serving someone who is."

The chain of thinking goes something like this, with more layers as the company gets larger and more complex: the *leader of managers* must focus his attention on the people he supports, the unit managers. The most important activity of the unit manager is to focus on the people she supports, the line employees. Next, the most crucial job of the line employees is to focus on serving the customer, specifically in the interactions which take place in the **magic square meter**. The logical conclusion then is that the most important focal point of the entire company is on people, whether the internal customer or the external ones.

This means that the *leader of managers* is actually a service provider, no matter how far away from the **magic square meter** she perceives herself to be in the system.

4

Be the Servant Leader

Let's go back to an earlier discussion and think about this statement again: every one of us, executive or dishwasher, starts the day by looking in the mirror at our reflection. The question the leader needs to ask at that moment is this, "What am I going to do today to make their jobs easier and more meaningful?"

This begs another question. How can you, the *leader of managers* in a competitive corporate environment begin to see yourself not as leader first, but as servant first? How do you change your outlook and behavior so that those you serve as a leader may themselves become **Servant Leaders**?

Of course, it helps to remind ourselves that we are in a "service industry." If you have followed this premise until now, you have considered my suggestion that your staff members are the ones who directly serve your customers, thus making your primary function supporting the people who work with you. Are you the leader who, like Ray Kroc, walks the perimeter of the parking lot and picks up trash, or who, like Ron Magruder the first President of Olive Garden, jumps behind the dish line during crunch time? Do you bus a table as you walk by, seat a party waiting at the desk, or ask the line cooks what they think about the work involved in prepping the new menu?

This might be a good moment to point out that the United States Marine Corps has as a core tenant—"officers eat last"—the strict cultural norm that an officer should take a meal only after her troops have been served first; in fact a chain ending with the highest ranking officer present. It is built on the simple principle that there is no need for officers if there are no front-line troops.

Robert K. Greenleaf, the long serving Director of Management Research at AT&T, first coined the phrase, "the Servant as Leader" in 1970. He spent the next twenty years of his life exploring this perspective.

Since then his influence can be seen in most, if not all, of the work done by the foremost management and leadership theorists of our time including Drucker, Blanchard, Kotter, Lawler, Handy and Buckingham. This is not the popular idea of the "inverted pyramid" putting customers at the top of the organization chart, but a deeper call to put the employee first—to serve as you lead.

Two New Perspectives

LEADER		SERVANT LEADER
• Change	←————→	• Direction
• Clarity	←————→	• Courage
• Focused on Collective Action	←————→	• Focused on a Shared Future

A lesson for the *leader of managers* can be learned from updating the ten principles Greenleaf proposed. These simple tenets align very well with the other lessons we have put forward throughout this book. The servant leader practices these things.

Listening and Understanding. In this the leader seeks to identify and clarify the will of the group, to hear what is necessary to serve them as they need to be served. At the same time, part of understanding is self-reflection, finding the inner voice that guides both personal growth and the ability to hear others. Listening and understanding are the two sides of other- and inner-directedness.

Acceptance and Empathy. The leader needs to recognize and accept in others their uniqueness and special talents. The servant leader projects and models their own good intentions by assuming the basic good intentions of others. All of us want to "have a good day at work" no matter at what level that work is being done. Empathy helps us see how we as leaders can make that possible. No leader can have empathy for others if she does not remember where her roots are—in the restaurant business you cannot forget what waiters and cooks do on every shift so the company can exist.

Conceptualization and Intuition. The servant leader needs to have the ability to think beyond the day to day realities of the organization and balance operational perspectives with a conceptual orientation. This also means nurturing employees to "dream great dreams" and stretch boundaries. Without ever having 100% of the necessary information for a decision, the leader needs to act on intuition, sometimes called judgment, to make calculated risks based on the information at hand. People want their leaders to have the big picture in mind so when they hear, "Let's go there" it is a natural choice to follow.

Foresight. As noted in the beginning of this chapter, the ability to foresee the likely outcome of a changing situation is a crucial component of leadership, it is called having vision. To understand the lessons from the past, the realities of the present and the likely consequences of actions in the future fosters trust in the leader from those he serves.

Awareness and Perception. A heightened sense of what is happening around them keeps the leader awake and energy-filled.

The intensity that comes from awareness, especially self-awareness, is not a comfort, but a challenge. This sense of self, and the perspective it opens, keeps leaders on edge. They are not satisfied, but disturbed, knowing that more needs to be accomplished, even while finding their own "inner serenity" enhanced during the stress brought on by the tasks ahead of them. This is where self-confidence shows and composure under pressure builds inner strength.

Persuasion and Consensus. There is a healthy reliance on persuasion for the servant leader, the ability to convince and not coerce the acceptance of ideas and vision. Effectiveness in building coalitions of support is more important than simple use of positional authority in making decisions within the organization.

Stewardship. The leader has a creative vision for the future and therefore must feel that there will be a better organization in place than the one they will leave behind. Servant leadership is about holding something in trust for another who will come later. Serving the developing needs of others, whether a new generation, the young manager being mentored, or the next unit to be opened, is all about a consideration of those yet to serve and those who will continue to lead into the future.

Commitment to the Growth of People. The leader as servant believes that people have an intrinsic value beyond their tangible contributions as workers. The organization which they lead will only become fully engaged when there is recognition of the tremendous responsibility to nurture the personal and professional growth of their employees.

Healing and Wholeness. For the *leader of managers*, this growth is exemplified by the concept of healing. Healing is the desire to "help make whole" those whom the servant leader encounters. It is driven in part and includes the need for wholeness and healing for the leader as well. As previously mentioned, we all want to say we had a good day at work, just as much as we want to work in a healthy and positive environment. The leader knows "I work here, too." The healing of relationships is a powerful force for transformation and integration, crucial aspects in the management of change.

Building Community. Organizations, sometimes small and intimate, sometimes large and mechanical, are the infrastructure of today's market economy. We all belong to many different organizations, but we spend the majority of our waking hours at work in a commercial organization. The servant leader knows that one of her most important roles is to re-establish the sense of small, local communities of employees, customers, and managers inside this larger, impersonal institution.

Epilogue

Keep this in mind: what makes you unique in the business environment is that your role is to lead the people who manage others.

This then is the plan for the *Leader of Managers*.

First, have a sense of your place in the history of the evolving marketplace, with a critical view of why multi-unit organizations have come to dominate the economic landscape.

Second, attain a strong sense of self-awareness with the individual skills and concepts necessary to succeed in this new multi-unit, multi-site, and multi-brand world. Model behavior and mentor others, take time to manage and to lead, and have personal control of your own development.

Third, conduct a comprehensive review of how the organization you lead is positioned to respond to the changing economy, especially focusing on the needs of the people in the organization. Great teams are forged on a foundation of individuals being encouraged to do more than they thought possible.

Fourth, embrace the four keys to success—becoming an **agent** of change, a **visionary** with a clear eye towards the future, a **champion** of the people who you have the responsibility to lead, and a **servant** first who serves so others may lead.

At the end of the day your job will be community building. Whether you call it networking, customer relationship marketing, employee retention, team-building or corporate social responsibility, ultimately what distinguishes the successful *leader of managers* from all others is the communities you create and the people you serve.

RESOURCES

Albrecht, Karl & Ron Zemke (1985) *Service America!*

Amabile, Teresa M. and Steven J. Kramer, Inner Work Life: Understanding the Subtext of Business Performance, *HBR*, May 2007

Birch, David. (1987). *Job Creation in America.* New York, Free Press

Blanchard, Ken and Phil Hodges, *The Servant Leader,* (2003), Nashville, Tenn., J. Countryman

Blau, Peter M. and Richard Scott (1962). *Formal Organizations.* San Francisco: Chandler

Boulgarides, J.D., & Rowe, A.J. (1983). Success patterns for women managers. *Business Forum*, 8(2), 22-24.

Buckingham, Marcus (2005) *The One Thing You Need to Know*, New York, Free Press

Campbell, D.F. (1994). *Critical Skills for Multi-Unit Restaurant Management.* Unpublished Monograph, Master's Thesis.

DiPietro, Robin B., Kevin S. Murphy,, Manuel Rivera and Christopher C. Muller, (2007), Multi-unit management key success factors in the casual dining restaurant industry: a case study, *International Journal of Contemporary Hospitality Management*

Drucker, Peter. (1955). *The Practice of Management.* London: Pan Books.

Drucker, Peter. (1985). *Innovation and Entrepreneurship*, New York, Harper & Row

Fayol, Henri. (1918). *Administration industrielle et generale; prevoyance, organisation, commandement, coordination, controle.* Dunot et Pinat, Paris.

Greenleaf, Robert K., (1970), *The Servant as Leader,* Indianapolis, IN, The Robert K. Greenleaf Center

Kakabadse, A., & Margerison, C. (1988). Top executives: Addressing their management development needs. *Leadership & Organization Development Journal*, 9(4), 17-21.

Kanter, Rosabeth Moss (2011) How Great Companies Think Differently, *Harvard Business Review*, November 2011

Kimberly, John R., and Robert H. Miles, and associates (1980) *The Organizational Life Cycle.* San Francisco; Jossey-Bass.

Lefever, M.M. (1989). Multi-unit management: Working your way up the corporate ladder. *The Cornell Hotel and Restaurant Administration Quarterly,* 30(1), 61-67.

Muller, C.C. (1999). The business of restaurants: 2001 and beyond. *International Journal of Hospitality Management*, 18(4), 401-413.

Muller, C.C., & Campbell, D.F. (1995). The attributes and attitudes of multiunit managers in a national quick-service restaurant firm. *Hospitality Research Journal,* 19(2), 3-19.

Muller, C.C., & Woods, R.H. (1994). An expanded restaurant typology. *The Cornell Hotel and Restaurant Administration Quarterly,* 35(3),

National Restaurant Association (2005). Restaurant Industry 2005 Fact Sheet. Retrieved on May 5, 2005 from http://www.restaurant.or/pdfs/research/2005factsheet.pdf

Paul, R.N. (1994). Status and outlook of the chain-restaurant industry. *The Cornell Hotel and Restaurant Administration Quarterly*, 35(3),

Pew Internet & American Life Project, July 11, 2011 http://pewinternet.org/Reports/2011/Smartphones.aspx

Reynolds, D. (2000). An exploratory investigation into behaviorally based success characteristics of foodservice managers. *Journal of Hospitality & Tourism Research,* 24(1).

Ritchie, B., & Riley, M. (2004). The role of the multi-unit manager within the strategy and structure relationship; evidence from the unexpected. *International Journal of Hospitality Management*, 23(2), 145-161.

Schein, Edgar H. (1985) *Organizational Culture and Leadership: A Dynamic View*. San Francisco, Jossey-Bass

Scott, William G. & Terence R. Mitchell, (1976). *Organization Theory*, Homewood, ILL: Richard D. Irwin Publishers

Griffith, Samuel B. translation (1971). *Sun Tzu, The Art of War*, New York, Oxford University Press

Technomics, Inc. (2004). 2004 Technomic Top 100 Report. Retrieved on May 5, 2005 from http://www.technomic.com/facts/top_100.html

Umbreit, W.T. (1989). Multiunit management: Managing at a distance. *The Cornell Hotel and Restaurant Administration Quarterly*, 30, 53-59.

Umbreit, W. T. (2001). Study of the changing role of multi-unit managers in quick service restaurant segment. In H.G. Parsa & F.A. Kwansa (Eds.), *Quick Service Restaurants, Franchising and Multi-Unit Chain Management* (pp.225-238). New York: The Haworth Hospitality Press.

Umbreit, W.T. & Smith, D.I. (1991). A study of the opinions and practices of successful multiunit fast service restaurant managers. *The Hospitality Research Journal,* 14, 451-458.

Umbreit, W.T., & Tomlin, J.W. (1986). Identifying and validating the job dimensions and task activities of multi-unit foodservice managers. *Proceedings of the 40th Annual Conference on Hotel, Restaurant, and Institutional Education*, August, 1986, pp. 66-72.

Van der Merwe, S. (1978). What personal attributes it takes to make it in management. *Ivey Business Quarterly*, 43(4), 28-32.

Woodward, Joan. (1965). *Analysis of Organizations, Industrial Organization: Theory and Practice.* New York, Oxford University Press

Wyckoff, D. Daryl & W. Earl Sasser(1978). *The Chain-Restaurant Industry* Lexington, MA, Lexington Books

About the Author

Christopher Muller, Ph.D. has focused his research on multi-unit restaurant brand management; chain restaurant organization development and growth; and the training of multi-unit managers for over 25 years.

Most recently he served as the Dean of Boston University's School of Hospitality Administration. Muller is often asked for commentary on hospitality, restaurant and travel issues in the national and trade press. He has appeared on ABC World News, CNN's "The Situation Room" & "Erin Burnett OutFront", USAToday, The New York Times, NPR, CBS Market Watch, The Wall Street Journal, as well as local print and broadcast media such as WCVB, WBUR, The Miami Herald and The Orlando Sentinel. He is a regular keynote and featured speaker at leading hospitality conferences.

Professor Muller is one of the co-founders of the annual European Foodservice Summit (www.efss.ch). Muller has lectured on management topics throughout the world, including Germany, Great Britain, Switzerland, Russia, Italy, Singapore, Hong Kong, Thailand, Korea, Australia, Mexico, Central and South America. Prior to Boston University he was a Professor in the Rosen College of Hospitality Management at the University of Central Florida where he was the Director of the Center for Multi-Unit Restaurant Management. Dr. Muller taught at Cornell University's School of Hospitality Administration for over a decade.

Dr. Muller co-founded 'Za-Bistro! Restaurant Holdings, Inc. a popular start-up restaurant company based in the Orlando, Florida market. He has worked in the international wine import and sales industry, and has served as a consultant to local, national and international restaurant, beverage, and hospitality management companies. He has been recognized as a Federal expert witness in a number of precedent setting legal cases on topics including restaurant trade dress and intellectual property, franchisee rights, and negligence issues.

He received both his Doctorate and Masters degrees from the School of Hotel Administration at Cornell University. Dr. Muller has published more than 30 articles in leading journals including *the Boston Hospitality Review, the International Journal of Hospitality Management, the Cornell Hotel and Restaurant Administration Quarterly, the Journal of Hospitality & Tourism Research, FIU Hospitality Review, Foodservice Europe*, and *the Hospitality and Tourism Educator.*

Made in the USA
Lexington, KY
19 February 2015